Modern Collector's Dolls

The current values in this book should be used only as a guide. They are not intended to set prices, which vary from one section of the country to another. Auction prices as well as dealer prices vary greatly and are affected by condition as well as demand. Neither the Author nor the Publisher assumes responsibility for any losses that might be incurred as a result of consulting this guide.

Printed by IMAGE GRAPHICS, Paducah, Kentucky

FOURTH SERIES
Modern Collector's Dolls

by

Patricia R. Smith

Published by

Collector Books

Box 3009 Paducah, Kentucky 42001

Distributed by

Crown Publishers, Inc.

One Park Ave.
New York, New York 10016

DEDICATION

This Volume IV in the Modern Series is dedicated to all who have helped put these volumes together, including the following who have helped with this book: Jayn Allen, Jane Alton, Frances Anicello, Joan Amundsen, Joan Asherbraner, Ruby K. Arnold, Sue Austin, John Axe, Yvonne Baird, Barbara Baker, Shirley Bertram, Mrs. E. Bethscheider, Joe Bourgious, Kay Bransky, Pat Burnell, Bessie Carson, Louise Ceglia, Connie Chase, Evelyn Chisman, Ruth Clark, Pearl Clasby, Evelyn Cline, Kathleen Flowers Council, Renie Culp, Edith DeAngelo, Sue Demerly, Jena Durham, Diane Duster, Helen Dyess, Marie Ernst, Kathryn Fain, Helen Faford, Irene Gann, Laura Gann, Lynn Gaudette, Mollye Goldman, Martha Gonyea, Jeanne Gregg, Eileen Harris, Gloria Harris, Sharon Hazel, Phyllis Houston, Ernestine Howard, Virginia Jones, Kimport Dolls, Betty Kirtley, Roberta Lago, Nancy Lucas, Steve Malicoat, Mandeville-Barkel, Marge Meisinger, Jay Minter, Connie Molak, Barbara Montezuzzi, Jan Morgan, Florence Black Musich, Jeanne Niswonger, Anita Pacey, Mary Partridge, Karen Penner, Carrie Perkins, Eveline Popp, Carolyn Powers, B. Schildes, Betty Snider, Sandy Rankow, Betty Tait, Kathy Walter, Ellie Watson, Emily Wolf, Loretta Zaboltny.

EDITOR: Karen Penner

All photographs by Dwight F. Smith, except for the Mandeville-Barkel Collection which was by Bob Gantz. Houston photos by Phyllis Houston, and all others credited with photo.

Other books by author:

Modern Collector's Dolls. Vol. I, II, & III
Antique Collector's Dolls. Vol. I & II
Armand Marseille Dolls
Kestner & Simon Halbig Dolls
Teen Dolls
Shirley Temple Dolls & Collectables, Vol. I & II
Madame Alexander Collector's Dolls
The Standard Modern Doll
The Standard Antique Doll
German Babies in Color
French Dolls in Color
Oriental Dolls in Color

CONTENTS

New and Revised Information

We try, in each volumne, to update information or to add new information for past volumes of the Modern Collector's Dolls series. The following are a few of these items.

In Series 111, on page 200 is a photo of an unidentified clown doll and Emily Wolf has sent information on her doll, which is in mint condition. An attached tag reads: A New Material Contents/Horsman Dolls, Inc./P.O. Box 1390/Columbia, S.C. 29202/Reg. No. Pa. 114 MASS. T-21. She describes the doll as seated, his face is sad. Held upright, his eyes slide forward and the mouth (chain) falls into a smile. He wears a red felt derby with blue flowers, blue felt pants with yellow suspenders over multi-plaid flannel coverall. White vinyl gloved hands and hair is yellow fake fur.

Esther Patterson has reported that she has a "Mary Jane" doll in the box. In Series 111, page 245, 265 Mary Jane is shown to be made by Togs & Dolls Corp. This company is listed in the National Directories (Registration) as being the makers but Esther's box reads: Mary Jane, Inc. and the clothes and panties have the name Mary Jane on them also. What we feel happened was that the 1954 Mary Jane, Inc. was licensed to Togs & Dolls in 1955. "Mary Jane" is also listed: #650700, filed July 1953 by G. H. & E. Freydberg, Inc. N.Y. So the mystery goes on!

The "Rosy Walker", page 223, Series 1 is owned by Patti Ann Pasquale and her doll is in the original box, has blonde hair and is marked American Character.

The Indian doll on page 41, Series 111 was made by Isleta Indians for the Tewa Weavers in Albuquerque. This information was sent by Dorothy G. Grooms.

Joan Amundsen sends information that she has a Danny O'Day with composition head that is dressed in a Texaco uniform, from the time that Jimmy Nelson did the commercials on the Milton Berle show on T.V.

Barbara Baker has the "Sweet Rosemary" doll shown on page 61 of Series 11 and reports her doll is also marked 251/AE 56, on her head. Her box says Betty The Beautiful Bride. Copyright Deluxe Premium Corp/Newark 4, N.J.

Advance Doll Company also made the Walking Wonder doll (Wanda and Winnie) in a bunny suit and her name was "The Walking Wabbit". Included with the doll was a mail order offer for dress/wig to change Wabbit into beautiful walking doll.

Phyllis Houston reports a doll with the marks: 15/6/Signature Doll/J/T 1969, on head. Body tag: Jolly Toys Inc./Skippy Doll Corp./Signature Doll Div./New York, N.Y. 10011. The Signature dolls were made by Jolly for the Montgomery Ward Co.

Mrs. Cindy Young sent information on the Dawn Series made by Deluxe Topper. She has six Dale dolls with bright pink lips instead of the light pink the others have. The costume and description is the same as the doll marked 4/H86, page 63, Series 111 only the six that she has marked: 4/H57, 4/H129, 4/H68, 4/H78, 4/H122, 4/H89. She has four additional Dale dolls and they are in different clothes and marked: 4/H111, 4/H137, 4/H57, 4/H84. The one with the H84 has green eyes to the left and pinkish-orange lips.

Cindy Young also reports that she has another Deluxe Topper Dawn series doll of interest. Her doll is marked 186/A11A but has short blonde hair, not straight but sort of page boy and also page boy type bangs. She looks older, in appearance, than the other youthful looking girls.

Kathryn Fain has been kind enough to share the following information with us: Page 230, Series 1 24" Suzy Smart was also sold as Susie Walker from the P.J. Hill Co. in Newark, N.J. Page 225, Series 1 the 19" Miss Glamour Ann dates from 1956 and was sold by Niresk Inc. of Chicago. She came with flower in hair and flowers at waist of dress. Had purse, trunk and 22 piece wardrobe. Page 222, Series 1. 15" World Traveler was also sold through Niresk Inc. dressed as Hollywood Bride. 1954. Came dressed as bride and had outfits of coat & beret, afternoon dress, hostess gown, plastic raincoat, ballet costume, sheer nightgown.

Kathryn Fain also reports that in Series 1, page 219 16" Crying Baby was also sold as Nu-Born Baby from the Novelty Mart in N.Y. in 1951. Dressed originally in nightie & diaper, wrapped in wool bunting with ribbon tie. Page 180, Series 11 the 16" Lili was sold from Doll-Land in Topeka in 1954. Came in laced-trimmed taffeta blouse, embossed design skirt.

It was reported in the Plaything magazine, May 5, 1976 that in Los Angeles a federal judge approved the $30 million settlement of class-action lawsuits against Mattel, Inc. that charged securities law violations.

Information from a doll box indicated that Marx is now a division of Quaker Oats Company. Courtesy Phyllis Houston.

18" "Margaret O'Brien" All composition and original. Alexander Doll Co. 1946. $200.00. (Courtesy Mandeville-Barkel Collection)

18" "Margaret O'Brien" All composition and original. 1947. $200.00. (Courtesy Roberta Lago)

18" "Louisa" 1952. One of the Alexander Doll Co. Fashions of the Century Series. All hard plastic. $85.00. (Courtesy Mary Partridge)

14" "Little Men" All hard plastic and original. Alexander Doll Co. 1952. $95.00. (Courtesy Mandeville-Barkel Collection)

16½" "Maggie Mixup" #1811-1960. Alexander Doll Co. $75.00. (Courtesy Carrie Perkins)

15" "Caroline" #4930-1961 and 21" "Jacqueline in an extra outfit of 1962. Alexander Doll Co. $125.00 & $250.00. (Courtesy Roberta Lago)

8" "Maggie Mixup" #611-1961. Alexander Doll Co. $60.00. (Courtesy Roberta Lago)

11" "Margot" #921-1961. Alexander Doll Co. $75.00. (Courtesy Carrie Perkins)

17" "Leslie" #1620-1966 and #1685-1967. This doll was never meant to be, nor marketed as the singer, Leslie Uggams. Alexander Doll Co. $65.00. (Courtesy Roberta Lago)

12" "Nancy Drew" #1262-1967. Alexander Doll Co. Wears linen shift dress under matching coat. $95.00. (Courtesy Mandeville-Barkel Collection)

14" "McGuffey Ana" #1450-1968. Plastic and vinyl. Alexander Doll Co. $45.00. (Courtesy Roberta Lago)

21" "Renoir Portrait" #2190-1972. Alexander Doll Co. $105.00. (Courtesy Roberta Lago)

16" "Kathleen" in green coat. She has brown eyes. The other doll is Sweet Sue with checkered headband. Dolls are made by the Princess Christine Doll Co. in West Germany. (Courtesy Anita Pacey)

16" "Jackie" with blue sleep eyes. He is all original and made in Germany by the Princess Christine Doll Co. (Courtesy Anita Pacey)

13" Same dolls by the West Germany Company of Princess Christine. The Black doll is Corina and the white one is Tommy. (Courtesy Anita Pacey)

11" "Southern Belle" #1185-1971. Alexander Doll Co.. $75.00. (Courtesy Mary Partridge)

3" "Tea Party Kiddles" Lady Lavender. (Courtesy Joan Ashabraner)

3" "Tea Party Kiddle" Lady Crimson. (Courtesy Joan Ashabraner)

18" "Mimi Bluette" from French movie and wears authentic costume from the movie. Very few have the fur boa.

18" "Contessa di Lyndon" played by actress, Marisa Berenson in movie Barry Lyndon. Authentic movie costume.

This is the MINT and original Shirley Temple Blue Bird doll. All composition. Originally in the Mandeville-Barkel collection, now in the Marge Meisinger Collection.

Shows the Shirley Temple Blue Bird doll in it's original box.

This is one of the more expensive dolls from the Furga Italy Company to show the quality of the clothing used. The basic dolls are the same. The older Furga's especially had fine clothing.

3" "Lady Silver" A Tea Party Kiddle. Marks: Mattel, Inc. 1967, on head. (Courtesy Joan Ashabraner)

This page shows the color pictures of a few of the creations, both made and designed, by Patricia Burnell. See other dolls by her under the section: Doll Artist. Left to right: Santa Claus, James Bond, Frankenstein and Clown.

8" COMPARISON STUDY

This is by no means a complete study of all the 7½" & 8" dolls but covers some of the most common hard plastic fashion dolls of the 1950's. Each one is deserving of it's own identity, as each had it's own personality.

PICTURE #1: 7½" "Janie" by Uneeda Doll Co. All three are Janie beginning with the earliest one. All are hard plastic with vinyl heads. All have large navels with middle high. 2nd & 3rd fingers are molded together. Molded black eyelashes, with three painted lashes at ends of eyes, except the first model, which is unpainted. Pug noses. Back of feet look like shoe seams but the front is plain without any detail. There is double crease at the ankles and the crease in the seat is Y and deeply molded. On the jointed knee dolls, the pins in the back of the legs can be clearly seen.

Uneeda--8" "Go Go" by Schiaparelli. This is the "Janie" doll with painted lashes. Vinyl head. Sleep blue eyes. (Courtesy Marge Meisinger)

Partial list of 7½" & 8" dolls:

ALEXANDER-KINS..Alexander	MISS ROSEUD..Rosebud, England
AMANDA JANE..England	MOLLEYE..Molly E Co.
BIG RED..Hollywood Doll	MUFFIE..Nancy Ann
BONITA..Allison Corp	NINNETTE..?
GIGI..A & H	PAM..Cosmopolitan
GINNY..Vogue	PAULA SUE..Ontario Plastics
GINGER..Cosmopolitan	PEGGY PETITE..Horsman
GOGO..Uneeda	PENNY..P.M.A.
JANIE..Uneeda	PLAYMATE..Virga/Beehler Arts
JANIE PIGTAILS..Uneeda	RANDI..Dutchess Doll
JEANETTE..Cosmopolitan	ROBERTA WALKER..Roberta
JOAN..P.M.A.	SANDRA SUE..Richwood
JOANIE PIGTAILS..P.M.A.	SHELLY ANN..Pedigree, England
JOHNNY..Roberta	SHERRY..Horsman
LORI ANN..Nancy Ann	TOMBOY..Japan
LUCY..Virga	VICKIE..P.M.A.
MAGGIE MIXUP..Alexander	VICKY..Unique
MARY LOU..Doll Bodies Inc.	WALKIN JOANIE..P.M.A.
MINDY..Active Doll Co.	WEE IMP..Vogue
MISS MEGOTOO..Aldens	WENDY..Alexander

Picture #2: All three dolls are 7½" "Ginger" by Cosmopolitan Doll Co. A mold seam runs through the middle of the ear, making the center part of the ear higher than top & lobe. Navel is faint. They have large round eyes but the very first ones had smaller eyes. There is a dimple under lower lip. Toes are all the same length and there are dots above the toes. The jointed knee model (3rd doll) has a crease in front at ankle high. All fingers are molded separately with a flaw at wrist on palms. There is fingernail and joint detail. The crease in the seat is flaired. Left to right: 7" early Ginger Walker with smaller eyes. 2nd issue Walker, only change is to larger eyes, 3rd is the 7½" Ginger with jointed knees. All three are completely hard plastic.

Cosmopolitan--7½" "Ginger" All hard plastic. Sleep blue eyes/molded lashes. Jointed knees. Walker. Marks: None. Original. (Courtesy Bessie Carson)

Cosmopolitan--7½" "Ginger" Close up of face.

Cosmopolitan--8" "Ginger" Hard plastic with vinyl head. Walker, head turns. All original. Paper purse with name. Marks: GINGER, on head. (Courtesy Bessie Carson). $7.00.

Cosmopolitan--8" "Ginger" Close up of face.

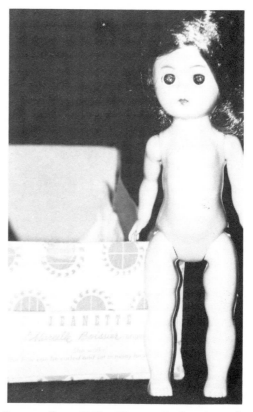

Terri Lee--Close up of the "Ginger" used by Terri Lee Co. for their "Scout" doll. $15.00.

Cosmopolitan--7½" "Jeanette" by Marcelle Boissier. This is Ginger, the 2nd issue. Was bought in quantity to distribute as Jeanette just as Terri Lee was purchased for their Scout dolls. (Courtesy Sharon Hazel). $10.00.

Cosmopolitan--7½" "Ginger" All hard plastic. Walker. Blue sleep eyes/molded lashes. Straight legs. Original. (Courtesy Bessie Carson). $10.00.

Cosmopolitan--1957 #4022 outfit for "Zippy". White felt pants. Red felt top/hat. Red shoes. Gold trim. Columbia Broadcasting Systems monkey and pet for "Ginger". Had six different outfits. $4.00.

Cosmopolitan--8" "Ginger" shown in original trunk/case with extra clothes, etc. (Courtesy Anita Pacey). $25.00.

Virga--This is "Lucy" hard plastic, shown in an original box. (Courtesy Marge Meisinger). $5.00 doll only - with case $15.00.

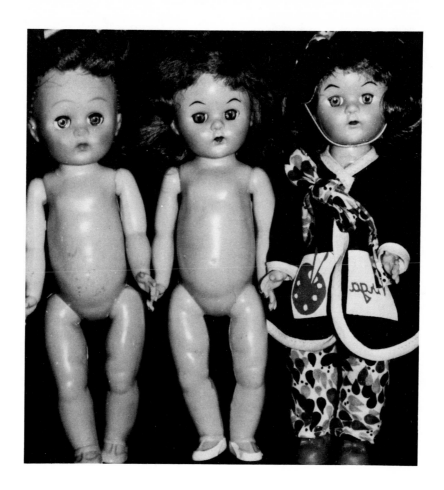

Picture #3: The first doll is 7½" "Pam" by Fortune Toys and ALSO "Lucy" (Virga) by Beehler Arts Co. These dolls were made by Ontario Plastics Inc. Rochester N.Y. and distributed by Plastic Molded Arts (called "Vicki"), Fortune & Beehler. Fortune Toys advertised their doll as "Pam, the Walking Fashion Plate" and Plastic Molded Arts, "Vicki, the doll with the FANTASTIC wardrobe" and within 2 years the Beehler Arts Co. started using vinyl heads (marked Virga) and one year later Plastic Molded Arts went to a vinyl head (marked Vicki), and the dolls went their separate ways. The third doll shown is a vinyl headed "Virga" (Lucy). All three Pam, Lucy or Virga, and Vicki have a longer, fatter body that has a crease in the seat with wide spread lines. ⋁ They have molded on T strap shoes (painted or unpainted) and a crease in the center of the knee cap. The seam lines cut through the back part of the ears. They have molded hair under the wigs. They have a deep indentation under the lower lip (no dimple). The 2nd & 3rd fingers are molded together.

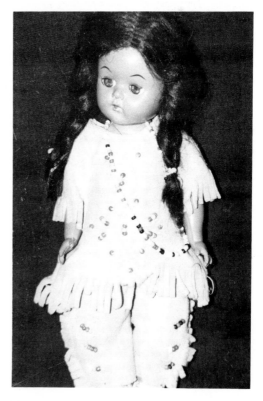

Virga--8" "Lucy" in original Indian outfit. (Courtesy Marge Meisinger) $8.00.

Fortune Toys--7½" "Pam" All hard plastic. Walker, head turns. Sleep blue eyes/molded lashes. Molded on T strap shoes. Shoes unpainted. Marks: None. (Courtesy Bessie Carson). $8.00.

Fortune Toys--Close up of "Pam" face.

Fortune Toys--7½" "Pam" with molded ballerina legs and feet. Very fine leg and toe detail. (Courtesy Jan Morgan). $10.00

Fortune Toys--7½" "Pam" with a vinyl head. Hard plastic body & limbs. Straight legs. Eyebrows are higher and mouth paint lighter than PMA'S Vicki. (Courtesy Sharon Hazel). $6.00.

Fortune Toys--This is close up of "Pam".

Left: Vinyl headed "Vicki" (incised). Right: "Pam, the Walking Fashion Plate". Head sits high on walker mechanism. Sleep eyes/molded lashes. Pug nose. Very good ear detail. High eyebrows. All fingers individual. Heavy seam lines down both sides of arms. Marks: PAM, on head. (Courtesy Sharon Hazel). $6.00.

Close up of Vicki with vinyl head. Marks: VICKI.

Shows close up of Pam, with vinyl head. Marks: PAM.

Picture #4: The first doll is "Gigi" by A & H Doll Mfg. Corp. Her head mold seam is in back of the ears. Her lashes are molded transparent. The crease in the seat is deep, Y and this area is molded higher. Excellent toe detail with two creases at the ankles. 2nd & 3rd fingers are molded together. There are black Gigi dolls. The 2nd doll is the very first Gigi with straight legs (one year only) and the description is same except she has painted on shoes with no indication of toes. The 3rd doll is "Petite Cheri" by Plastic Molded Arts (came in 10" chubby size also). This 7½" size has no lashes. The mold seam is behind the ears & she has a double crease below the knees & at the front of the ankles, also a two line crease at the elbow joint. There is good toe detail. She is hip pinned walker & her head turns. All three dolls are completely hard plastic.

A & H--7½" "Gigi" All hard plastic. Jointed knees. Red glued on wig. Marks: None. (Courtesy Bessie Carson). $7.00.

A & H--Close up of "Gigi" face.

A & H--Right: 7½" "Gigi" with a vinyl head. Body is hard plastic and same construction as full hard plastic dolls. Sleep eyes with lashes painted under eyes only. Left: This is "Mindy" by Active Doll Corp., the same Ginger doll used by many different companies, all purchased from Cosmopolitan. (Courtesy Sharon Hazel). $6.00.

Close up of another Ginger face, this time as Active Doll Corp.'s "Mindy".

A & H--8" "Gigi" Shown in an original outfit and with an original box. (Courtesy Marge Meisinger). $12.00.

Picture #5: This first doll is 7" "Jeanie" by Roberta Doll Co. The boy version is called "Johnny". Some of the bodies are marked: A Product of Doll Bodies Inc/New York N.Y. The molded lashes are so heavy that the eyes only open part way. Not a walker. They have painted on shoes with bows in the front. She looks more like Vogue's Ginny than the others. The 2nd doll is 7½" "Nancy Ann" (Lori Ann) by Nancy Ann Storybook Doll Co. She has the same body construction as their Muffie doll, which is usually marked. I am sure she has replaced arms so I won't describe them. She has a vinyl head, with eyelashes painted above. Her head is marked Nancy Ann. The 3rd doll is 8½" "Pam" by Fortune Toys with molded ballerina feet. She is an all hard plastic walker & her head turns. $4.00 - $10.00 -$10.00.

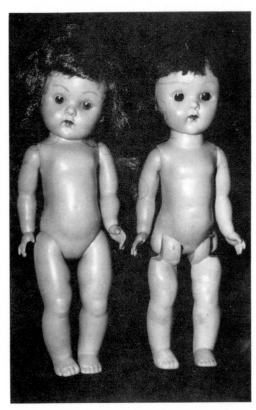

Vogue--8" "Ginny" All hard plastic. Left is the first hard plastic with straight legs, non-walker and has no lashes. Right is first walker, who also has no lashes. $22.00 - $20.00.

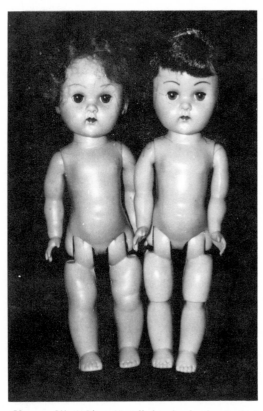

Vogue--8" "Ginny" All hard plastic. Left is straight leg walker with molded lashes. Right is the bend knee walker with molded lashes. $16.00 -$12.00.

Nancy Ann--7½" "Lori Ann" Hard plastic with vinyl head. Walker, head turns. Sleep blue eyes/molded lashes. Marks: NANCY ANN, on head. STORYBOOK DOLLS/CALIFORNIA/MUFFIE, on back. (Courtesy Bessie Carson). $10.00.

Nancy Ann--7½" "Lori Ann" Close up of face.

Nancy Ann--7½" "Lori Ann" Early one. Brown eyes/ molded lashes. No painted ones. All vinyl. Red hair. Original. Marks: NANCY ANN, on head. (Courtesy Bessie Carson). $9.00.

Nancy Ann--7½" "Muffie" All hard plastic. This is an early one with no brows or lashes, painted ones only. Sleep blue eyes. Paper tag on wrist: 500/MUFFIE. STORYBOOK/DOLLS /CALIFORNIA, on back. Original. (Courtesy Bessie Carson). $15.00.

Nancy Ann--7½" "Muffie" Close up of face.

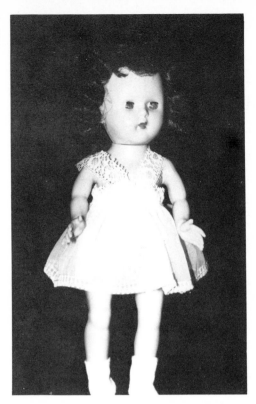

Hollywood Doll--8" "Little Red" All hard plastic. Sleep eyes with molded black lashes. Marks: $15.00.

A HOLLYWOOD DOLL
TRADEMARK
1947

Allison Corp.--8" "Bonita" All hard plastic. Delicate finger with 2nd & 3rd molded together. Sleep eyes with molded lashes. Smile mouth. Some body seam lines are heavy. Excellent quality head. $10.00.

Roberta--8½" "Roberta Walker" All hard plastic. One in original clothes and wig. Other to show construction. Molded hair under wig. Deep knee dimples. Very good toe detail. Walkers, head turn. Marks: None. (Courtesy Bessie Carson). $7.00.

Plastic Molded Arts--10½" "Sandy" All hard plastic. Blue sleep eyes. Walker, head turns. Marks: PLASTIC MOLDED ARTS/L.I.C. NEW YORK, on back. Original dress. $7.00.

England--7½" "Miss Rosebud" Ginny type doll. Originally dressed as "Woman of Holland, Denmark". All hard plastic. Blue sleep eyes. Has bent legs of a baby. Marks: MISS ROSEBUD/MADE IN ENGLAND. (Courtesy Karen Penner). $7.00.

Left: 8" "Paula Sue" All hard plastic. Sleep eyes with molded lashes. Deep nose mold and cleft under the nose. Made in Canada by and marked: Ontario Plastics Inc. Rochester N.Y. Right: 7½" "Amanda Jane" Body & legs are rigid plastic. Head & arms are vinyl. Dark pink skin tones. Large sleep brown eyes/long lashes. Small "Rosebud" mouth. Marks: MADE IN ENGLAND, on head. MADE IN ENGLAND/AMANDA/JANE. (Courtesy Sharon Hazel). $10.00 - $7.00.

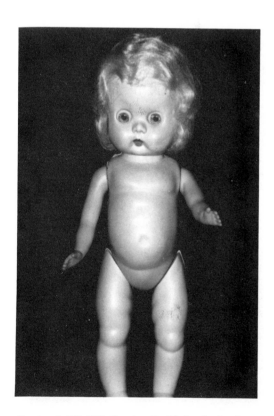

England--8" "Shelly Ann" All hard plastic except arms that are vinyl. Pale blue sleep eyes with clear plastic molded lashes. Head and legs are strung. No neck, head fits flush onto body. Glued on mohair wig. Marks: MADE IN ENGLAND, on back 3, inside arms. Made by Pedigree. $7.00.

19

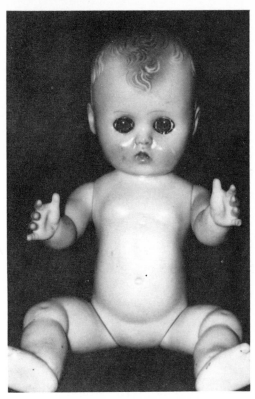

Nancy Ann--10" "Baby" All vinyl. Open mouth/nurser. Blue sleep eyes. Marks: NANCY ANN, on head. $12.00.

7½" "Ginger Baby" All vinyl with sleep eyes/molded lashes. Crease under breasts. Mold hole not cut out in small of back with wetting hole located between legs. Rooted hair. (Courtesy Sharon Hazel). $8.00.

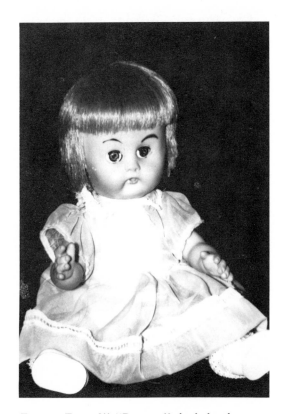

8" Gigi's "Lil' Sister" Painted vinyl body & limbs. Vinyl head with receded chin. Nurser. Very large sleep eyes/molded lashes. Partly separated toes on right foot. 2nd & 3rd fingers molded together on right hand. Molded light brown hair. Marks: GIGI'S/LIL SISTER. $8.00

Fortune Toys--8" "Pamette" the baby that goes with "Pam". 1957. All vinyl. Sleep blue eyes/long lashes. Black brows. Open mouth/nurser. Receded chin. Original. Marks: 36, on head. $5.00

Active Dolls--7" "British Princess" All hard plastic with one piece body and legs. Brown mohair wig. Pink gown with darker pink ribbon. Gold crown. Marks: None. 1953. $4.00.

Active Dolls--10½" "Queen" All hard plastic with one piece body and legs. Gold print with rose shawl and gold crown. Has Star of David necklace. 1956. $4.00. (Photo courtesy Carolyn Powers)

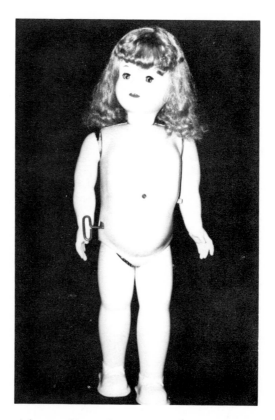

Advance--24" Talking & walking "Winnie, the Wonder Doll". All hard plastic. Open mouth with two upper teeth. Sleep blue eyes/lashes. Roller on non-removable shoes for walking. Key wind with start & stop button on opposite side. Very large "barral" chest area for talking mechanism. 1957. $55.00.

Advance--Shows body view of 24" "Wanda Talker & Walker".

11" "Carmen" All composition with tin sleep eyes and closed mouth. Original. Collectors call these dolls "Carmen Miranda" but they were never marketed under that name. 1937. $100.00 (Courtesy Jeanne Niswonger)

The Alexander Doll Company began in 1923, with Madame Alexander making all cloth dolls and by the 1930's she was creating costumed composition dolls. It was the end of 1940's that this company began using the hard plastics and the quality of the Alexander hard plastic dolls are among the finest.

In the modern field, Madame Alexander dolls are considered to be the most collectable because everyone wants them. But dealers and collectors should be aware that the outrageous prices being asked for, and paid, is extremely mint dolls, that is dolls that have been unplayed with/in original condition with box. A great amount of the Alexanders were "play" dolls and will be found in various conditions. Many of these play dolls are nude and you will never know who they are (personality) unless you have the original clothes or can check the hairstyle with an original one. Needless to say, just because the doll is marked "Alexander" and is nude or redressed, this does not mean that she will be worth as much as an all original one.

Because we have completed an all Alexander Doll book (Madame Alexander's Collectors Dolls) just a short time ago, the dolls shown in this section are duplicates from that book. The all Alexander book contains over 1000 dolls with over 340 pages, so it was impossible to come up with different dolls for this section in such a short time. BUT, these dolls are not duplicates from the previous Modern Collector's Dolls series.

9" "McGuffey Ana" All composition with painted features. Original wig and clothes. 1935-39. $75.00. (Courtesy Jeanne Niswonger)

Alexander--14" "Jo", of Little Women using Maggie faced hard plastic doll. The doll is unmarked and clothes are tagged with white/red letter label. Gown is gaberdine that is red with blue velvet "bib". $75.00. (Courtesy Elizabeth Montesano of Yesterdays Children)

Alexander--14" "Polly Pigtails" All hard plastic and using the Maggie face doll. Sleep eyes and original. $95.00. (Courtesy B. Schilde)

Alexander--14" "Polly Pigtails" shown in plaid, original dress. $95.00. (Courtesy John Axe)

Alexander--17" "Margaret O'Brien" All hard plastic with red mohair wig with loop braids tied with a ribbon. Original dress and pinafore but missing hat. $185.00. (Courtesy Sandy Rankow)

Alexander--18" "Maggie Walker" All hard plastic and original. Carries original suitcase with comb, brush and curlers. Rhinestones on skirt. $75.00. (Courtesy Sandy Rankow)

Alexander--21" "Cissy" All hard plastic with vinyl oversleeve arms. Jointed elbows and knees. Yellow satin dress and matching coat. $75.00. (Courtesy Sandy Rankow)

Alexander-9" "Little Southern Girl" Magic skin latex body and limbs in one piece. Jointed neck with vinyl head. Glued on brown wig and painted features. Marks: Alexander, on head. Clothes are tagged. 1951. $55.00. (Courtesy Phyllis Houston)

Alexander--9½" "Margot" All hard plastic using the Cissette doll. The Margot and Jacqueline dolls have special eye treatment with blue eyelids (some Portrette, also). This doll is #921-1961. $115.00 (Courtesy Jeanne Niswonger)

Alexander--This photo shows two Cissettes with some of the Alexander doll furniture. (Courtesy Jeanne Niswonger)

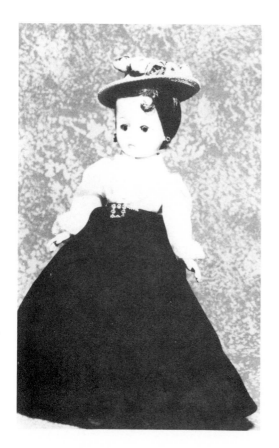

Alexander--10'' Cissettte as "Gibson Girl". All hard plastic with the Margot hairstyle. Black skirt and white blouse. Jointed knees. 1962. $300.00. (Courtesy Jeanne Niswonger).

Alexander--10'' "Cissette" in the International outfit of Iceland. 1961. All hard plastic. Jointed knees. $300.00. (Courtesy Jeanne Niswonger).

Alexander--8" "Little Tiny Billie Toddler" to show the body construction. 1953-54 only. $85.00. (Courtesy Jeannie Niswonger)

Alexander--8" "Southern Belle" 1956. All hard plastic, jointed knee walker. Original. Marks: Alex., on back. Gown tagged: Madame Alexander, etc. $200.00. (Courtesy Jeanne Niswonger)

Alexander--8" "Little Melanie" #411-1954. The gown is pale blue with a natural straw hat. $165.00 (Courtesy Jeanne Niswonger)

Alexander--8" "Wendy Ann" (Alexander-kins) in outfit #556-1956. Two piece felt. $65.00. (Courtesy Jeanne Niswonger)

Alexander--8'' ''Alexanderkin'' in outfit #541-1956 with bathing suit, beach robe and bonnet. Bag and sun glasses. $65.00. (Courtesy Jeanne Niswonger)

Alexander--8'' ''Billy'' and ''Wendy'' Dressed in outfit #420-1959 and #432-1959. $85.00. & $65.00. (Courtesy Jeanne Niswonger)

Alexander--8'' ''Alexanderkins'' in skating outfit #540-1959. One piece bodysuit and blouse. Felt skirt, shoe ice skates. $85.00. (Courtesy Jeanne Niswonger)

Alexander--8'' ''Wendy'' Alexander-kins dressed in #423-1961 tennis outfit and carries toy tennis racket. $85.00. (Courtesy Jeanne Niswonger)

Alexander--8" "Southern Belle" #385-1963. Satin gown with rows of lace and matching bonnet. $165.00. (Courtesy Jeanne Niswonger)

Alexander--8" Alexander-kins "Ballerina" #620-1965. Sequined bodice. Came in pink, blue and yellow. $65.00. (Courtesy Jeanne Niswonger)

Alexander--8" Alexander-kins dressed in outfit #0621-1965. $65.00. (Courtesy Connie Chase)

Alexander--12" "Lissy" in the special FOA Scwartz Anniversary outfit of "Katie" 1962. A very rare doll. $200.00. (Courtesy Marge Meisinger)

Alexander--"Lissy" dressed as one of the Little Women, Amy. 1964. All hard plastic with jointed knees and elbows. $65.00. (Courtesy Jeanne Niswonger)

Alexander--"Lissy" as Pamela of 1966. All hard plastic. Takes wigs and dressed in Polish costume. Sold as boxed set, with wig changes thro FOA Swartz. $125.00. (Courtesy Jeanne Niswonger)

Alexander--12" "Kathy Cry Dolly" Blonde rooted hair over molded forehead curl. Open mouth/nurser. All vinyl and original. $45.00. (Courtesy Evelyn Cline)

Alexander--17" "Marlo Thomas"-That Girl (T.V. Show) #1789-1967. All original. $350.00. (Courtesy Jeanne Niswonger)

Alexander--12'' ''Janie Ballerina'' (replaced shoes). #1124-1965. Pink sequined bodice with rhinestones on skirt. Marks: Alexander 1964, on head. $55.00.

Alexander--12'' ''Laurie'' of Little Women. #1226-1967 to date. Still available. (Courtesy Jeanne Niswonger)

Alexander--21'' ''Scarlett O'Hara'' Portrait of 1975-76. Green satin gown and matching bonnet with white lace trim. Marks: Alexander-1961. $100.00. (Courtesy Phyllis Houston)

Alexander--This shows the body construction of the early 21'' Portraits. It uses the Cissy body with vinyl oversleeve arms and jointed elbows. The remainder of the body is hard plastic and she has jointed knees.

AMERICAN CHARACTER DOLL COMPANY

The American Character Doll Company dates from 1918 and the early dolls were marked Aceedeecee (trademark for their composition) and later the dolls were marked Petite. From the late 1930's until the company went out of business in 1968, the dolls are marked with the full company name or just Amer. Char. straight and later in a circle.

The American Doll and Toy Corp. was originally it's own company and began in the late 1890's with S.D. Hoffman and his "Can't Break 'em" process for composition. In 1909-1910 this company and process for composition was sold to the Aetna Company that later became the Horsman process (on merger). The name American Doll and Toy Corp. was revived and used by American Character Doll Company from 1959

(1960) to the date the company was sold in 1968. During these years the company ran an International Import Division.

The dolls imported by American Character (American Doll & Toy) were and are still very much collector's items. These dolls came from Italo-Cremona of Italy, Ratti and Valenzasca, also from Italy and the Luigi Furga Company. Poupee's Bella of Terignan, France. Rheinische Gummi Und. Celuloid Fabrik of Mannheim Germany. Casseloid Company from Leicester, England.

All American Character (American Doll & Toy) have fine quality and had as much "character" as any American manufacturer. All the dolls from this company are highly collectable.

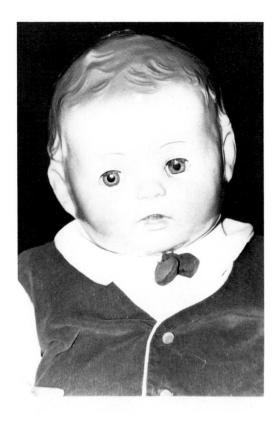

American Character--18" "Baby Sandy" All rubber body and limbs (jointed) with composition head. Sleep tin eyes/lashes. Open mouth with tongue. Marks: PETITE, on head. 1937. $125.00. (Courtesy Connie Chase)

American Character--21" "Sunny Boy" Cloth body with early vinyl arms, legs and head. Open/closed mouth, inset blue eyes and molded hair. 1951. $45.00.

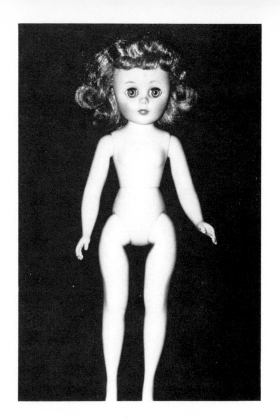

American Character--16" "Barbara Sue" All vinyl with one piece body and legs. Arms are disk jointed. She has a pouty, worried expression. All original. Marks: Amer. Char. Doll, on head. 1955. $35.00. (Courtesy Phyllis Houston)

American Character--13" All rigid vinyl with jointed waist. Sleep eyes, medium heel feet and pale nail polish. Used both as Sweet Sue and Toni. Marks: None. 1957. $25.00. (Courtesy Marie Ernst)

American Character--14½" "Sweet Sue" All hard plastic. Sleep blue eyes/lashes. Closed mouth. Original dress, shoes and hat. 1957. $35.00. (Courtesy Kathy Walker)

American Character--15" Left: "Baby Toodles" All excellent quality heavy vinyl. Molded brown hair. Sleep blue eyes. Separate large toes and all fingers. Marks: AMERICAN CHARACTER DOLL CORP./1958, on head. Right: Good quality rigid plastic with vinyl head. Individual toes and fingers. Sleep blue eyes. Marks: 63, on head. $22.00-$15.00. (Courtesy Marie Ernst)

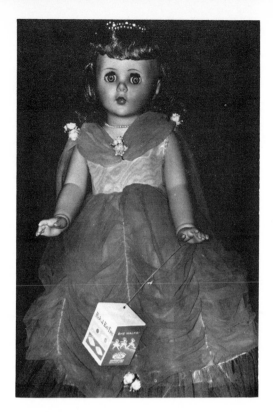

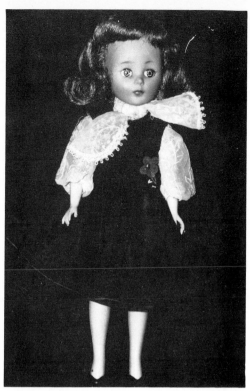

American Character--25" "Sweet Sue" with "peek-a-boo" eyes that are the type that follow you without moving from side to side. She has the Toodle Lou arms and hands. Original. Marks: American Character/1960, on head. $120.00. (Courtesy Anita Pacey)

American Character--10" "Toni" All vinyl with flanged joints. Sleep blue eyes/molded lashes. Original (except shoes). Marks: 1958. $25.00. (Courtesy Marie Ernst)

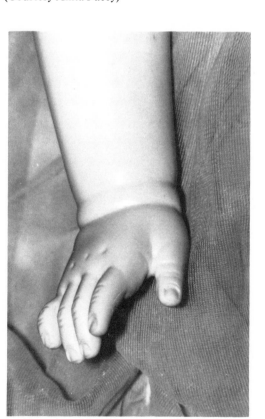

American Character--Shows a close up of the hands on the large 25" Sweet Sue dolls. This same hand and wrist is the style used on other dolls from this company, such as the Toodl-Lou series.

American Character--11½" "Poppi" All plastic. Pops apart at the waist and the bust. High heels. Vinyl wigs and has small painted brown eyes with molded lashes. Cut out clothes are of vinyl-plastic. 1961. Marks: None. $9.00. (Courtesy Phyllis Houston)

American Character--11½" "Darlin' Dollface" All vinyl with open/closed mouth. Rooted hair. Sleep eyes. Marks: AMER. CHAR. INC./1965, on head. $15.00. (Courtesy Phyllis Houston)

American Character--19" "Pretty Penny" All rigid plastic with vinyl head seated into body. Sleep "follow" eyes/long lashes. Posable arms are strung. During the 1960's the American Character Doll Co. was exclusive import dealers for several European doll companies and this doll is one of the results. Marks: Amer. Char. Co/1966, on head. "Bella"/Made in France Brevete SGDG, on back. $45.00.

American Character--Shows the body and hands of the 19" American Character and Bella of France doll.

AMSCO--14" "Polly Pretend" Plastic and vinyl with decal type brown eyes. Open/closed mouth. Comes with "mothers" clothing as she "pretends" to be grownup. Designed by Marvin Glass & Ass'ts. Marks: AMSCO/1974, on head. Came in white version also. Original. White $12.00. Black $16.00.

ARRANBEE DOLL COMPANY

The Arranbee Doll Company was founded in 1922 and was purchased by the Vogue Doll Company in 1959. Vogue discontinued with the use of the name "Arranbee-R & B" in 1961.

The hard plastics made by Arranbee rate very high, both in beauty and also in quality. These hard plastic dolls are either marked R & B or just Made in USA on the back or with mold #210.

AMSCO--9" "Superbabies" Captain America, with removable mitts and shield & bonnet. Batman has freckles. Vinyl heads with painted features and rooted hair. Cloth bodies. Marks: AMSCO Ind./Div. of Milton Bradley Co/etc., on tag. Made in/Hong Kong, on head. $6.00.

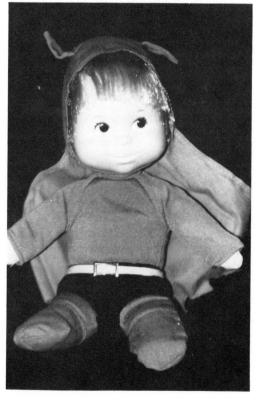

9" Superbaby Batman. Same description as Captain America. $6.00.

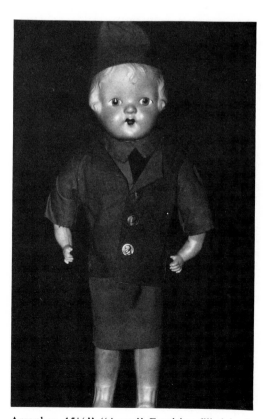

Arranbee--15½" "Army" Excelsior filled body with composition arms, legs and head. Painted blue eyes and molded hair. Original army color uniform with replica Lincoln pennies for buttons. Marks: None. Circa 1930. $65.00. (Courtesy Kay Bransky)

35

Arranbee--15" Excelsior filled body with composition arms, legs and head. Painted on black shoes. Molded hair and painted blue eyes. See following photo for mark on body. 1934. $65.00. (Courtesy Kay Bransky)

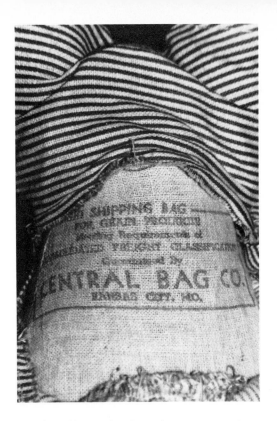

Arranbee--Shows the Central Bag Co. mark on body. Dolls made by Arranbee for their employees during the early 1930's.

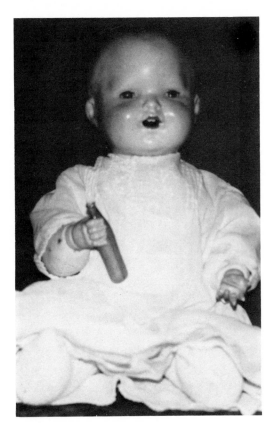

Arranbee--18" "Original Bottletot" Composition head, cloth body with both celluloid hands. The celluloid bottle is attached to hand. Open mouth and smile eyes. 1935. $45.00. (Courtesy Mary Partridge)

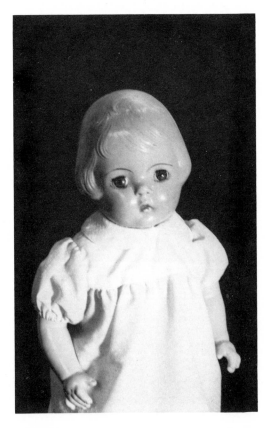

Arranbee--19" "Rosie" Cloth body with composition swivel head on composition shoulder plate. Composition arms and legs. Pin disc joints. Legs are long and straight. Brown sleep eyes. Molded hair. Open/closed mouth. Marks: AR-RANBEE. 1935. $26.00. (Courtesy Phyllis Houston)

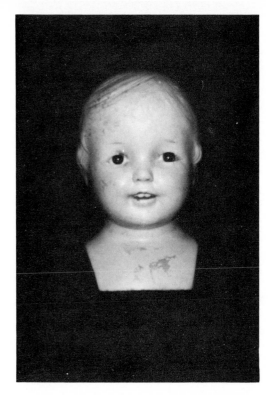

Arranbee--7" tall head. "Nancy" (Came in marked wardrobe case). Fibroid type composition shoulder head. Open mouth with four teeth and tongue. Date unknown. Complete doll $35.00. (Photo courtesy Carolyn Powers)

Arranbee--14" "Nancy Lee" All composition with sleep eyes and dark eyeshadow. Human hair wig and all original. 1939. $45.00. (Courtesy Mandeville-Barkel Collection)

Arranbee--18" "Princess Betty Rose" All composition with thin face and limbs. Large brown sleep eyes and closed mouth. Human hair wig. Original gown is yellow net-like material. 1938. Marks: R & B, on head. $65.00. (Photo courtesy Barbara Baker)

Arranbee--15" "Scarlet" (Nancy Lee). All composition with green sleep eyes/lashes and black eyeshadow. Closed mouth. Original. Marks: R & B, on head. 1940. $45.00. (Courtesy Kimport Dolls)

Arranbee--20" "Carolyn the Snow Queen" 1940. All composition with bent right arm, blonde mohair wig, blue sleep eyes/lashes. Original except replaced tiara. Marks: Faint R & B, on head. Same doll was issued as Miss Marie in 1942-43. $55.00.

Arranbee--21" "Nancy Jean" All composition. All jointed. Original blonde human hair wig. Painted mouth. Blue sleep eyes, grey shadow. Original socks and very unusual shoes. Marks: R&B, on head. Clothes not original. $65.00. (Courtesy Austin Colllection)

Arranbee--17" "Nancy Lee" 1951. All hard plastic with glued on saran wig in ponytail. Original. Marks: R & B, on head. $45.00. (Courtesy Mary Partridge)

Arranbee--17" "Nancy Lee" 1952. All hard plastic. Nylon yarn hair in pulled back hairdo. Original yellow-gold ballerina outfit. (Author). $65.00.

Arranbee--14" "Bride" (Nanette) All hard plastic with blue sleep eyes/lashes. Original. 1953-54. $45.00. (Courtesy Mary Partridge)

Arranbee--14" "Nancy Lee" Heavy, excellent quality vinyl. Sleep blue eyes/lashes. Painted lashes under eyes only. Closed mouth. Distinctive eyebrows. 1954. Marks: Arranbee, on head. (Author). $65.00.

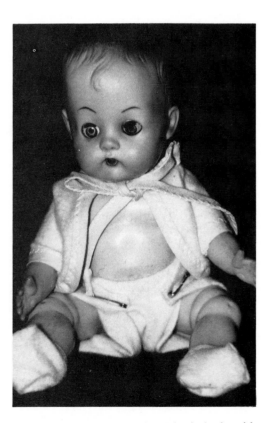

Arranbee--8" "Baby Marie" Plastic body with vinyl arms, legs and head. Sleep blue eyes with molded lashes. Molded hair. Excellent ear detail. Open mouth/nurser. Small indent on head looks like "R". Made for Kresges Stores. 1963. $4.00. (Courtesy Sharon Hazel)

Arco--5" "John-John" This is actually a ceramic figurine but many collector's include these figures among their dolls. Printed on bottom: 1963 AR-CO/Cleve. Ohio/E 1844. $15.00. (Photo courtesy Florence Black Musich)

Arrow--4" "Yuk" All vinyl that is orange/yellow. Bright green sleep eye. Marks: PAT. PEND/ARROW INDUSTRIES, on head. 13, in square on back. Circa 1965. $4.00. (Courtesy Phyllis Houston)

Baby Berry--13" "Lil Abner" and 12" "Daisy Mae". Daisy has one piece vinyl body and limbs. Blue sleep eyes & rooted hair. Molded bust. Marks: Exclusive License/Baby Berry/Toy N.Y.C./Al Capp/Dog Patch Family, on tag. Lil Abner is constructed the same with molded hair and painted features. His vinyl shoes are much larger than his feet. Marks: B.B. Doll, on shoes. Baby Berry Doll/25 1957, on head. Lil Abner $65.00. Daisy $65.00. (Courtesy Helen Dyess)

Baby Berry--13" "Mammy" and "Pappy Yokum". Mammy has one piece body and limbs with a very large molded bust. Marks: N.Y. Doll Co. 3C, on shoes. B.B. 25, on head. Al Capp/Dog Patch Family/Exclusive License/Baby Berry/Toy N.Y.C., on tag. Pappy also has one piece body and limbs. Marks: Same as Mammy except B.B. Doll, on shoes. Mammy $75.00. Pappy $75.00. (Courtesy Helen Dyess)

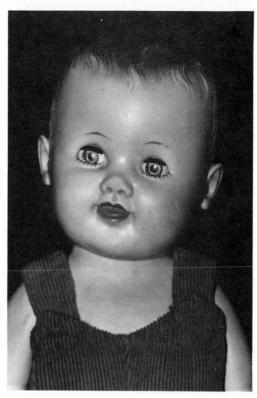

Baby Berry--21'' ''Mammy Yokum'' Heavy stuffed vinyl head and gauntlet hands. Glued on yarn wig. Cloth body and limbs. Original felt clothes. Marks: Baby Berry/1952, on head. $95.00. (Courtesy Betty Kirtley)

Belle--13½'' ''Jackie'' Heavy one piece stuffed body and limbs. Good toe detail and detail of separate fingers. Vinyl head. Molded hair. Excellent ear detail. Sleep, smiling blue eyes/lashes. Painted lashes under eyes only. Open/closed mouth. Marks: 14, on head. 1954. $14.00.

Belle--10'' ''Little Miss Margie'' All rigid vinyl with jointed waist. Sleep blue eyes. Marks: Ⓟ . Belle Doll & Toy Corp., on box. This same doll and mold was used by several different companies. 1957. $6.00. (Courtesy Marie Ernst)

Berman & Anderson--10'' ''Laurel'' and ''Hardy'' All vinyl with molded on shoes, and hats. Painted features. Original. Made by the Berman & Anderson Co. 1973. $8.00 each. (Courtesy Jay Minter)

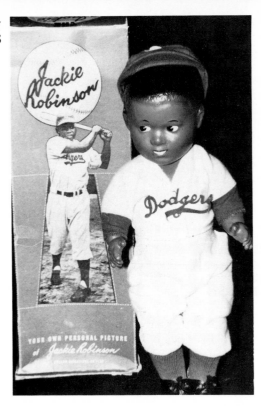

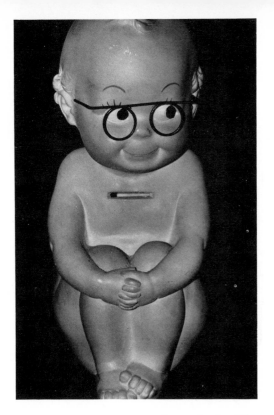

Bradsby Co.--13'' ''Jackie Robinson'' All composition with painted features. Shown with original box. Marks: None. Louisville slugger/bats/Hillerich S. Bradsby & Co./Louisville, KY. 1950. $135.00. (Courtesy Jay Minter)

Brooks--11½'' One piece plaster bank. Wire glasses. Good detail and has molded wings. Marks: Official Thinking Kewpie. A.N. Brooks Corp./Merchandise Mart/Chicago, IL. USA 1966. $10.00.

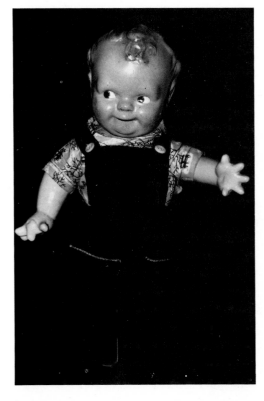

Cameo--15'' ''Skootles'' All composition jointed at neck, hips and shoulders. Painted features and molded hair. 1930's. $145.00. (Courtesy Jay Minter)

10'' ''Campbell Kids'' Special offer for BiCentennal. All vinyl dolls. 1976. $12.00 each. (Courtesy Connie Chase)

Castle--8" "Castle Collection" Fashions from American History. Plastic with rigid vinyl heads. All very good quality dolls and clothes. Sleep eyes/molded brown lashes. Marks: Made in Hong Kong, on head and backs. Clockwise: Scarlet, Ginny, Priscilla, Mary Louise, Betsy and Christine. 1975. $5.00 each.

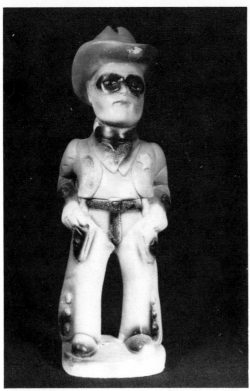

Chalk--16'' ''Lone Ranger'' All chalk. Given at carnivals during the 1930's. $20.00. (Courtesy Phyllis Houston)

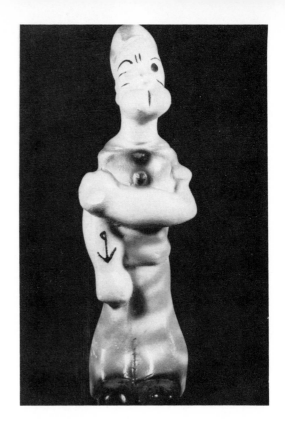

Chalk--16'' Chalk ''Popeye'' (pipe is missing) All chalk, painted. Given at carnivals during the 1930's. $20.00. (Courtesy Phyllis Houston)

Chalk--8'' ''Grumpy'' All chalk with sprinkled on glitter. Given at carnivals during the 1930's. $6.00. (Courtesy Phyllis Houston)

Chalk--16'' ''Snow White'' All chalk, painted with sprinkled on glitter. Given at carnivals during the 1930's. $20.00. (Courtesy Phyllis Houston)

Chrysler Corp.--9" "Mr. Fleet" All one piece vinyl with slot in head back, for bank. Marks: CHRYSLER CORPORATION/1973 Made in U.S.A., on bottom. $4.00.

Cloth--18" Lithographed doll in peasant costume. Colors are red, black and white. No tags. $4.00. (Courtesy Phyllis Houston)

Cloth--11½" "China" and "Cherie", the French doll. Dolls of the Allies. All felt. Marks: Dolls of the Allies, created & designed by Ern Westmore/famous motion picture/make-up artist. Made in California, Belgium, China, England, Czechoslavakia, France, Greece, Hawaii, Holland, Norway, Poland, Russia, U.S.A., on tag. My Country was invaded on June 14, 1940 & now I am an orphan. Will you please adopt me?, on France tag. $8.00 each. (Courtesy Pearl Clasby)

Cloth--9½" Stuffed cloth over bendable wire frames. She is very pregnant and he is quite insoucient. Sparse wigs are glued on. Marks: None. Date unknown. $25.00 pair. (Courtesy Phyllis Houston)

45

Cloth--4½" Trio of "Dwarfs" Lithographed cloth. Marks: None. Came with 15" Snow White. Cut & sew/set of 1963. $3.00 each. (Courtesy Phyllis Houston)

Cloth--19" "Raggedy Ann" This is an older one with tin button eyes. $8.00.

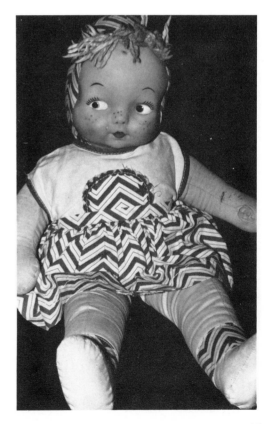

Cloth--18" "Honey Lou" Vinyl face mask with blue eyes painted to the side. Yellow yarn hair. All cloth body with oil cloth feet. Freckles on nose and cheeks. Original dress, bonnet missing. Marks: 054 DOLL, on base of neck. Honey Lou/135491-135492 Pat. Pend./Gund Mfg. Co. J. Swedlin Ind. 1951. $6.00. (Courtesy Marie Ernst)

Cloth--14" "Nancy" All cloth with Buckram face mask. "Fur" hair. Marks: None. $22.00. (Courtesy Kimport Dolls)

Cloth--22" All cloth with lithographed features. Felt ears and removable top. Excelsior filled. Chun-Kee stamped on top. $3.00. (Courtesy Joan Amundsen)

Cloth--34" All cloth "Alice In Wonderland" Body and limbs of peach color muslin. Face is stiffened cloth mask and painted features. Yarn hair. $45.00. (Courtesy Phyllis Houston)

Cloth--Ad for 36'' tall cowboy from a 1952 sewing magazine. $25.00.

Cloth--Shows ad for a 36'' all felt ballerina. 1952. $25.00.

Cloth--10'' "Play Angel" All felt with velour face. Wired arms. Marks: CLARE/CREATIONS, INC., on tag. 1970. $2.00.

Cloth--13'' "Kangeroo/Family" Lithographed cloth. Home made. 1971. $4.00.

Cloth--9½'' ''Red Riding Hood'' 10'' ''Wolf''
All printed cloth. She has removable skirt and
cape. Wolf has removable cape. Comes with
cloth bed with canopy and book. Marks: QUESTER
EDUCATION PRODUCTS, INC., on tag. 1975.
$16.00.

Cloth--9½'' ''Cinderella'' and 10½'' ''Prince
Charming'' All printed cloth. Removable skirt
and extra dress for her, removable hat for him.
Came with pumpkin/coach, book, pail & broom.
Marks: QUESTER EDUCATION PRODUCTS,
INC., on tag. 1975. $16.00.

Cloth--9½'' ''Mary Had A Little Lamb'' All
cloth that is printed. Removable skirt and hats.
School pillow and book. Marks: QUESTER
EDUCATION PRODUCTS, INC., on tag. 1975.
$16.00.

Cloth--18'' Lithographed all cloth doll from the
Aunt Sarah's Pancake Houses of Richmond, Va.
1975. $3.00. (Courtesy Phyllis Houston)

College House--7" Vinyl "Head Cheerleader" In-set eyes. Fake fur body. Original. One in a series. 1966. Marks: The Campus Kids/College House/381 4th Ave./NYC, NY., on box. $4.00. (Photo courtesy Florence Black Musich)

Cosmopolitan--9" "Japan Girl" of dress-me type as a Japanese. Orange, gold, beige and brown costume with yellow plastic shoes! Black glued on wig, sleep eyes, fully jointed. One of a series that included Scotch, Italian, Polish, Alaskan, Spanish, etc. Marks: None except on package. 1960. $5.00. (Courtesy Phyllis Houston)

David, C.A.--17" "Unknown Personality" Plastic with vinyl head and arms. Has molded on mustache. Marks: C.A. DAVID/1967, on head. 17BST, on upper arms. $75.00. (Courtesy Jayn Allen)

David, C.A.--17" "Unknown Personality" Plastic with vinyl head and arms. Open/closed mouth. Very character face. Rooted hair. Marks: C.A. David/1967, on head. 17BST, on upper arms. $65.00. (Courtesy Jayn Allen)

DELUXE TOYS

Deluxe Toys is the parent company for: Deluxe Reading, Deluxe Topper, Topper Corp., Topper Toys and Deluxe Toy Creations. All are the same company. These companies are no longer in business.

Most of their dolls are marked with one of the above names, but they made many dolls just marked with an "AE" and number following that.

Deluxe--20" "Candy Fashion" All vinyl with jointed elbows and knees. Marks: A1 HH K92, on head (One seen also marked-A1 HH K 70). Sleep blue eyes, pierced ears and human hair. 1957. $30.00 complete. (Courtesy Carolyn Powers)

Deluxe--This shows the case and the insides of the case holding the 20" Candy Doll and the three extra dresses that are with her. (Photo courtesy Carolyn Powers)

Deluxe--25" "Sweet Janie" 1959. Rigid vinyl with vinyl head. Sleep blue eyes/lashes. Closed mouth. Jointed waist. Original. Marks: 190, on head. Deluxe Premium, on box. $20.00. (Courtesy Anita Pacey)

51

DeSoto--23'' ''Heart Beat Baby'' Painted hard plastic head. Cloth body with latex arms & legs. Sleep blue eyes/lashes. Glued on saran wig over molded hair. Cryer box in back, lay her down and heart beats. Marks: An original DeSoto/Creation, on tag. Wears heart necklace. 1951. $25.00. (Courtesy Betty Snider)

DeSoto Dolls--14'' ''Bride'' All hard plastic with sleep blue eyes/lashes. Painted lashes below eyes only. Closed mouth. Original. Marks: MADE IN U.S.A., on back. 14, on head. DeSoto Doll/DeSoto Mfg. Co. Chicago, Ill., on tag. 1954. $22.00. (Courtesy Betty Snider)

Disney, Walt--12'' ''Pinocchio'' All composition with elbows and knees to look like they are jointed. Original felt and cotton clothes. Marks: Pinocchio/WD Pr. Knickerbocher Toy Co., on head. Pinocchio/W.D. Pr. KN. Toy/U.S.A., on back. $55.00. (Courtesy Phyllis Houston)

Disney--9'' Tall to tip of horn. ''Ferdinand'' All composition and fully jointed with pipecleaner and string tail. Marks: Ferdinand, over right front leg. W.D. Ent./Ideal Novelty/& Toy Co./Made in U.S.A., over right rear leg. $55.00. (Courtesy Jena Durham)

Disney--10'' ''Mickey Mouse'' Stuffed rolly polly body with vinyl head mask & vinyl ears. Felt hands and feet. Marks: M. Mouse/Walt Disney Prod./Gund Mfg. Co., on tag. $10.00. (Courtesy Mary Partridge)

Disney--5½'' ''Mickey Mouse'' All bendable vinyl. All clothes molded on. Marks: (C) WALT DISNEY/PRODUCTIONS HONG KONG, on seat of pants. Came stapled to a card. $2.00. (Courtesy Phyllis Houston)

Disney--10'' (including ears!) ''Mickey Mouse Hobo'' with polka dotted bag over shoulder. All vinyl with no moving parts. A Squeaky toy. $4.00. (Courtesy Phyllis Houston)

Disney--10'' (including ears!) ''Mickey Mouse'' with polka dotted bag over shoulder. All vinyl with only moving part his swivel head. A squeaky toy. Marks: DELL/(C) Walt Disney Prod., on right foot. $6.00. (Courtesy Phyllis Houston)

Disney, Walt--8½" "Minnie Mouse" (Left) Wood filled velvet with felt hands. Non-removable dress. Circa late 1940's. Marks: Walt Disney Prod. Wood Bey Products/Made in Japan, on tag. $7.00. 9½" "Minnie Mouse" (Right) Foam stuffed cloth body, fleece arms and feet. Removable dress. Elastic in head to hang doll. Marks: WDP, on head. Minnie Mouse/Copyright Walt Disney Prod./Gind Mfg. Co., on tag. 1958. $6.00. (Both courtesy Mary Partridge)

Disney--8" (includes ears) "Mickey Mouse" All vinyl and usual jointing. Vinyl shoes and cotton suit. Marks: (C) Walt Disney/Production/R Dakin & Company/Product of Hong Kong., on bottom of each foot. MICKEY MOUSE/ Walt/Disney/Productions, on tag. Clothing tag also. 1975. $3.00. (Courtesy Phyllis Houston)

Disney, Walt--11" "Minnie Mouse" Good quality plastic with molded on clothing. Vinyl, turning head. Has single wheel set into each foot and cupped hands. She originally was pushing a baby carriage. Marks: Walt Disney/Productions, on back. $9.00. (Courtesy Phyllis Houston)

Disney, Walt--6" "Minnie Mouse" Plastic & vinyl. Removable clothes & vinyl ribbon. Marks: WALT DISNEY/PRODUCTIONS, on head. R. DAKIN & COMPANY, on tag. 1973. $3.00.

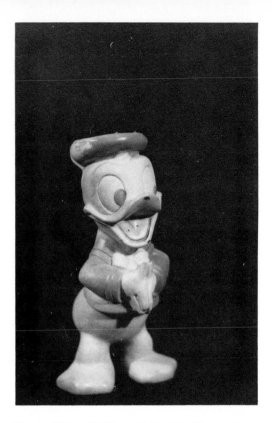

Disney, Walt--6" "Donald Duck" All one piece, brightly painted vinyl. Marks: Dell/Walt Disney Prod., on bottom of right foot. $4.00. (Courtesy Phyllis Houston)

Disney, Walt--10" "Donald Duck" One piece squeaky toy. Marks: Walt Disney Prod/The Sun Rubber Co/Barberton O U.S.A./29. $10.00. (Courtesy Phyllis Houston)

Disney--10½" "Donald Duck" with binoculars. (Bird or girl-watching??). Head swivels, rest in one piece. All vinyl. A squeaky toy. Marks: DELL/(C) Walt Disney Prod., on right foot. $4.00. (Courtesy Phyllis Houston)

Disney, Walt--11" "Donald Duck" Roly-poly that is all plastic and musical. Marks: None. $5.00. (Courtesy Phyllis Houston)

Disney, Walt-- 8" "Donald Duck" Plastic & vinyl. Removable clothes. Marks: WALT DISNEY PRODUCTIONS, on head. PRODUCT OF HONG KONG, on bottom of feet. R. DAKIN & CO., on tag. 1973. $3.00.

Disney, Walt--8½" "Dopey" Plush filled with vinyl head. Marks: W.D.P., on head. Dopey/The Wonderful World/Of Gundikins/Gund. $6.00. (Courtesy Mary Partridge)

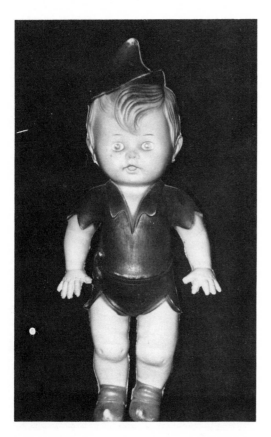

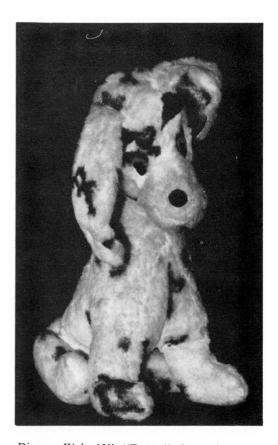

Disney, Walt--9½" "Peter Pan" All one piece vinyl with molded on clothes. Open/closed mouth. Marks: Peter Pan/W. Disney Prod./The Sun Rubber Co./Barberton, Ohio U.S.A. $10.00. (Courtesy Mary Partridge)

Disney, Walt--13" "Tramp" from the movie "Lady and the Tramp". $5.00.

Disney, Walt--12" "Pluto (Tip of tail to tip of nose) Fully jointed. Vinyl and plastic. Separate collar. Marks: Walt Disney Productions/R. Dakin & Company/Product of Hong Kong. 1975. $3.00. (Courtesy Phyllis Houston)

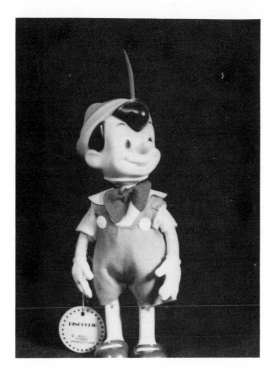

Disney--8" "Pinocchio" Rigid vinyl body and legs; softer vinyl head and arms. Usual jointing although knees LOOK like they are jointed also -they aren't. Molded on hat with feather, molded on gloves, slip-on shoes. Cotton suit. Marks: (C) WALT DISNEY/PRODUC-TIONS/R. Dakin and Co./Product of Hong Kong, on each foot. Cardboard label and also a cloth label sewn to clothing. 1975. $3.00. (Courtesy Phyllis Houston)

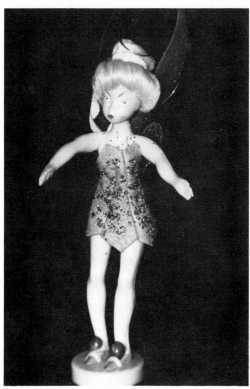

Disney, Walt--6" "Tinkerbell" All one piece (except head) bendable wired vinyl. Glued on wig. Original. Marks: BENDY, on back Plastic wings. $8.00. (Courtesy Connie Chase)

Disney, Walt--5' and 3' figures on motorcycles made for Disneyworld as part of an antimated group from the movie "Bedknobs and Broomsticks". The 18 figures and 6 animals of the group have been released to collectors. $1000.00. (Courtesy Kimport Dolls)

Once in a great while a truley original and exceptionally fine artist appears, and in this case it is Patricia Burnell of California.

Pat fully researches her dolls and spends much time at libraries, not only to research the character, but also the correct design of the clothing.

Pat's dolls heads, hands and feet are sculptured of clay composition, then fired. She has no molds and each doll is hand done and an original work. The bodies are covered wire armitures that are posable in any position.

To be able to add one of Pat Burnell's dolls to your collection would be a joy indeed as she is really a fine artist and her dolls will, one day, rate as high as a fine quality French doll does now.

Doll Artist--13½'' ''Witch'' Made by Pat Burnell
and her personal favorite. $265.00.

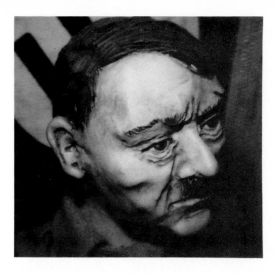

Doll Artist--14½'' ''Hitler'' By Pat Burnell. $265.00.

Doll Artist--14'' Close up of the face of ''Emmett Kelly'' made by Pat Burnell. $225.00.

Doll Artist--14½'' ''Apple Granny'' By Pat Burnell. $225.00.

Doll Artist--15'' ''Mexican Macho'' By Pat Burnell. $250.00.

Doll Artist--14'' ''Eskimo'' with close up of face.
Made by Pat Burnell. $265.00.

Doll Artist--15'' ''Arab'' By Pat Burnell. $250.00.

Doll Artist--15" "Gippeto" and tiny "Pinocchio" with close up of face. Made by Pat Burnell. $285.00.

Doll Artist--16" "Man", 14½" "Woman", 9½" "Boy" and 6½" "Girl" Made by Pat Burnell. $235.00 each.

Doll Artist--16½" Close up of head of Abe Lincoln. By Pat Burnell. $225.00.

Doll Artist--15½'' ''Indian and Child'' Made by Pat Burnell, including gun. $285.00.

Doll Artist--10½'' ''Irish Leperchane'' Red fur wig. Made by Pat Burnell. $195.00.

Doll Artist--16'' ''Scotsman'' with natural red fur wig. $195.00. (Courtesy Pat Burnell)

Doll Artist--16'' ''Viking'' Made by Pat Burnell, including all weapons and hat. $285.00.

Doll Artist--15½'' ''Mongol Pirate'' Made by Pat Burnell. $265.00.

Doll Artist--16'' ''Ghengas Khan'' Designed and made by Pat Burnell. $265.00.

Doll Artist--15'' (standing) ''Gypsy'' By Pat Burnell. $250.00.

Doll Artist--15½'' ''Genie'' Coming from his bottle. Made by Pat Burnell. $225.00.

Doll Artist--16" "Organ Grinder" Holding little Stieff monkey. Doll made by Pat Burnell. $250.00.

Doll Artist--11" "Gandalf The Gray" From the book "The Hobbit" by Tolkin. Made by Pat Burnell. $285.00.

Doll Artist--16" "Moroni" A book of Morman figure. Holding the Golden Plates, later translated into "The Book of Morman" by Pat Burnell. $265.00.

Doll Artist--15½" "Pirate" By Pat Burnell. $265.00.

Doll Artist--15" "Chinese Worker" By Pat Burnell. $225.00.

Wooden portrait doll by Maxine Clasen. No jointing at neck. Arms are wire and cloth with wooden hands. Portrait of John Houston. (I do believe Maxine could be set down in the middle of the desert and she'd find something out of which to make a doll!) Face is a good likeness. $60.00. (Courtesy Phyllis Houston)

Artist's Doll--36" "Scout" By Maxine Clasen. This is supposed to be our son John as a cub scout. There is a heavy armature with cloth covering, making the doll fully posable. Molded and painted hair, painted eyes (very fine). Head and hands are composition. $120.00. (Courtesy Phyllis Houston).

Doll Artist--This boy & girl were designed and created by Barbara Ferry. $55.00 each. (Photo courtesy Ellie Watson)

Doll Artist--These delightful young children are the creations of Barbara Ferry. $55.00 each. (Photo courtesy Ellie Watson)

Doll Artist--21'' ''Amanda'' and ''Sal'' with silk face, yarn hair and button eyes. An all original design and made by Lynn Gaudette. $65.00 each.

Doll Artist--21'' ''Tomblina'' With blue sleep eyes. All original with original dress design. Made by Lynn Gaudette. $65.00.

Doll Artist--21" "Stumbles" With dark sleep eyes. Another Lynn Gaudette original. $75.00.

Doll Artist--22" "Negro Ladies" Made and designed by Martha Gonyea. Photo's also by Martha Gonyea.

Doll Artist--22" "Indian Maid" A design of Martha Gonyea.

Doll Artist--22" "Fiesta Lady" All original and made by Martha Gonyea.

Doll Artist--22" "Fiesta Lady" Made and designed by Martha Gonyea.

Doll Artist--22" "Indian Maids" Original design of Martha Gonyea.

Doll Artist-- 21" "Rag Shirley Temple" Designed and made by Sue Austin 1977. Embroidered features including dimples. Over 50 individually crochetted curls. Red/white dress, felt shoes, white cotton undies trimmed with lace. (Photo courtesy Larry Zwolinski). (Doll courtesy Austin Collection).

Doll Artist--16" "Rag Baseball Player" #4 designed and made by Sue Austin in 1976 to celebrate her son Phil's 16-0 season. Authentic navy/white uniform including brim hat and spiked felt shoes. Felt features and yarn hair. (Photo courtesy Larry Zwolinski) (Doll courtesy Austin Collection)

17" "Nun Doll" (Dominican Order) $28.00.
18" "Gibson Girl" $35.00. Both of these made of white porcelain. Hand painted facial features. Made and costumed by Emily Wolf. (Photo courtesy E.L. Vandiver)

Doll Artist--9'' ''Lura Isabella'' with little girl ''Cindy Lou'' and doll. Stocking over wire armature. Painted features. Marks: The Lura Doll, on tag. $55.00. (Courtesy Anita Pacey)

Doll Artist--19'' ''1776 Bicentennial Doll'' All especially formed and processed cloth doll. Made by Maria Smith. $95.00. (Courtesy Anita Pacey)

Doll Artist--19'' ''George and Martha Washington'' Stuffed cloth with stitched faces. Made by Maria Smith. $65.00. (Courtesy Anita Pacey)

Doll Artist--13½'' ''Betsy Ross'' Made by Estella E. Stensgaard, who owned the Wilshire Doll Hospital in Los Angeles. 1934. Plaster type shoulder head, arms and legs. Painted features. Red mohair wig. Cloth body, upper arms and legs. Flag has 13 stars. The tiny scissors actually work. She sits in red chair, also made by Mrs. Stensgaard. $145.00. (Photo courtesy Helen Dyess)

Doll Artist--18" "Mark" Doll #151. Made in 1976 from a photograph by Eveline Popp. $95.00.

Doll Artist--18" Oriental baby made from a photograph. Doll is #156. Made by Eveline Popp. 1976. $95.00.

Doll Artist--6" Tall "Boy Scout, Cub Scout and Campfire Girl" All made by Mary Alice Volek. $6.00 each. (Courtesy Gloria Harris)

Doll Artist--13" "Minute Man" A Bicentennial wax created by Doll Artist Shelia Wallace. Embedded hair on head, arms, eyebrows, lashes and chest. Limited edition. $200.00.

Doll Artist--This is another model of the dolls (Limited number) made by Miss Mary Hortence Webster, assisted by Laredo Taft. 1920's. $95.00. (Photo courtesy Marge Meisinger)

Doll Artist--28'' ''Flapper'' Doll made by Miss Mary Hortence Webster (Assisted by sculptor Loredo Taft) 1920-1925. Only 20 were made and given as gifts. Some smaller ones were made and sold through Marshall Fields for about $25.00 during the 1920's. $95.00. (Photo courtesy Marge Meisinger)

Doll Artist--5'' Tall with 7¾'' circumference Agatha and called ''Witch Agatha'' because the Huron, Ohio Regional had a program on witchcraft and this was the head given at that Regional (Summer 1976). Marks: AGATHA/L.W. 1975,/Circle C, on shoulder. Made by N.I.A.D.A. Doll Artist, Lita Wilson. $85.00.

Doll Artist--4'' Clothespin-wax head ''Peddler'' doll created by Barbara Wright. Based on an article in an English magazine. $45.00. (Photo courtesy Ellie Watson)

Doll Artist--1¼" Tiny, tiny "Teddy" minature, hand carved in wood with painted red heart. By Connie Molak.

DOLL ARTIST

Connie Molak is a wooden doll maker, member of International Doll Makers and because the carving is a long tedious process will never be able to "mass" produce her dolls. The collector who has one of her dolls will admit that the wait to receive the doll was worth it. Connie is a former art teacher and is now housewife and mother of five children.

Doll Artist--2" Tiny "Teddy" Hand carved of wood with red painted heart. By Connie Molak.

Doll Artist--2" "Child with Teddy Bear" Hand carved miniture by Connie Molak.

Doll Artist--15" Tall and 14" side to side. "The Hobbit" taken from Tolkiens "Hobbit" hand carved of wood and oil painted with inset glass eyes. By Connie Molak.

Doll Artist--China that was the 1960 United Federation of Doll Clubs convention doll. $65.00. (Courtesy Kimport Dolls)

Doll Artist--9" Cloth bodies with straight bisque arms and legs. Bisque heads with large painted eyes. Glued on mohair wigs. Maker unknown. $20.00 each. (Courtesy Kimport Dolls)

Durham--18" "Charly" A new girl in town. Plastic with vinyl arms and head. Painted blue eyes. Rooted yellow hair. Marks: None on doll. Durham, on box. Re-issued 1976-1977. (Courtesy Joe Bougious)

Durham--8¾" "M.A.S.H." figures. All rigid vinyl with molded hair. Dressed in molded on uniforms under clothes. Push button in back moves arms. Marks: 1969 Aspen Productions, on box. Durham Industries, Inc. and rest is rubbed out, on bodies. $4.00. (Courtesy Virginia Jones)

The name of this company is made up from the name of the owner and founder, E.G. Goldberger. The company was founded in 1917 and the early dolls were marked E.G., then later E. Goldberger and now Eegee.

Eegee--19" "My Fair Lady" All vinyl with jointed waist. Red fingernails. Sleep blue eyes/lashes & black eyeshadow. Pierced ears, high heels and rooted light brown hair. Original black & white dress/hat. Designed for Eegee by Mollye Goldman. Marks: 14R, on head. 1956 C.B.S. Inc., on box. Looks just like Broadway star inspired by Broadway hit show "My Fair Lady". $75.00. (Courtesy Marie Ernst)

Eegee--13" "Merry Stroller" Hard plastic body and limbs. Pin hipped walker. Vinyl head with sleep blue eyes/lashes. Original in suitcase. Marks: Eegee, on head. 1957. $28.00 with trunk. (Courtesy Anita Pacey)

Eegee--20" "Little Debutante Ballerina" Hard plastic walker with non-turning head. Jointed knees and ankles, waist. Vinyl arms and head. Sleep blue eyes. Back of head molded flat. Marks: 14R, on head. 1958. $16.00. (Courtesy Marie Ernst)

Eegee--15" "Playtime Susan" All good quality vinyl. Open mouth/nurser, sleep eyes, molded hair, spread fingers with hands toward body. Probably original dress. Marks: EEGEE, on head. 1960. $6.00. (Courtesy Phyllis Houston)

Eegee--4½" "Nurse" All vinyl with one piece body, legs and arms. Painted eyes. Marks: EEGEE CO., on head and body. Circa 1965. $2.00. (Courtesy Marie Ernst)

Eegee--12" "Baby Luv" Cloth with vinyl limbs and head. Large painted eyes, rooted hair and smile mouth. Marks: 14BT/Eegee Co. 1973. $28.00. (Courtesy Anita Pacey)

Eegee--22'' ''Cinderella Handee Poppett'' Vinyl head with remainder cloth puppet body and limbs. Open/closed mouth. Heavy molded lashes. Painted eyes. Pink rooted hair. Marks: EEGEE/1974/POL, on neck. $18.00. (Courtesy Phyllis Houston)

Eegee--14'' ''Maskerade Magic'' Cloth with removable skirt only. Vinyl head and gauntlet hands. Painted features. Comes with five plastic masks: Nurse, Bride, Movie Star, Princess and Majorette. Marks: EEGEE CO./12D, on head. Goldberger, on tag. (Eegee). 1976. $8.00.

Since the Alexander dolls have increased at such a fast rate, price wise, Effanbee dolls have become even more collectable, due to this, we have decided to show collectors a cross section and variation that collecting Effanbee dolls can achieve.

Effanbee is the original company started by Bernard E. Fleischaker and Hugo Baum in 1910. The Noma Company that makes Christmas Tree ornaments bought Effanbee in 1947 but sold it back to one of the sons of the founders, Walter Fleischaker and two partners. They ran the company until 1971 when it was sold again.

Dolls are marked Effanbee or F & B and a few may be found with what appears to be a mis-spelling but is not: Effandbee.

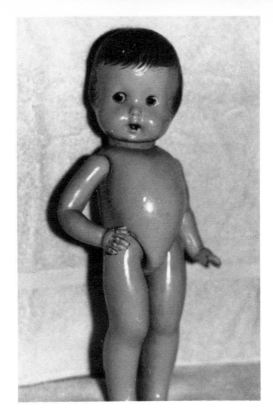

Effanbee--14'' ''Catherine'' All composition with molded red hair and round, painted eyes. Patsy body. 1927. $75.00. (Photo courtesy Shirley Bertram)

Effanbee--16'' Two faced child. Cloth body with celluloid head with two faces and molded tears on one side. Redressed. Marks: F & B, on head. $165.00. (Courtesy Sandy Rankow)

Effanbee--13" "Baby Wonder" All composition with sleep tin eyes/lashes. Open/closed mouth and inset celluloid left hand and bottle. 1935. $45.00.

Effanbee--11½" "Patsy Jr." All composition with painted, molded hair and painted eyes. All original. Marks: Effanbee/Patsy Jr./Doll, on body. Childhood doll of Melissa Middleton Mandeville. 1931-32. $60.00. (Courtesy Mandeville-Barkel Collection)

Effanbee--14" "1620-Plymouth Colony Effanbee Historical Doll" Grey with white collar, cuffs and apron. All composition doll with painted brown eyes. Marks: Effanbee, on head. 1939. $200.00. (Courtesy Jay Minter)

Effanbee--18" "Today's Girl" 1943. Pink cloth body, arms and legs with baby style composition hands that have pink nail polish. Composition head with painted eyes. Black yarn hair. White blouse with royal blue, full legged pants. Red sash. Head is attached with wooden plug. Marks: None. $80.00. (Courtesy Marie Ernst)

Effanbee--11" "Nurse-1938-41" All composition with molded, painted hair. Sold with set of five babies. Also sold as Jolly Joan Waitress from 1940 to 1941 (Portland, Oregon). $65.00. (Courtesy Ruby K. Arnold)

Effanbee--19" "Baby Bright Eyes" Cloth body with composition head, arms and legs. Blue sleep eyes/lashes. Molded and painted hair. Closed mouth. Clothes not original. Marks: Effanbee/19-- (can't read last two numbers). 1946. $65.00. (Courtesy Phyllis Houston)

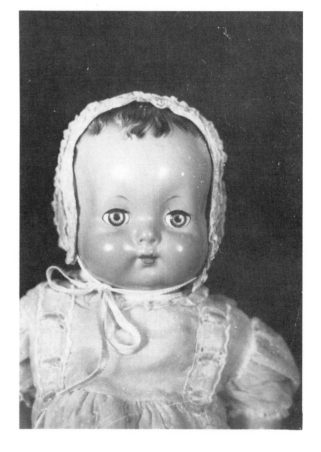

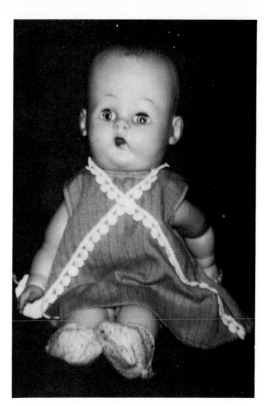

Effanbee--8½'' ''Patsy Babyettes'' All composition with wigs over molded hair. Sleep blue eyes. Came in gift box set. He is original, she is not. Marks: Effanbee/Patsy Babyette, on backs. 1947. $50.00 each. (Courtesy Jay Minter)

Effanbee--13½'' ''Dy-Dee Baby'' One piece stuffed vinyl body and legs. Disk jointed stuffed vinyl arms. Vinyl head with open/closed mouth and sleep blue eyes. Marks: Effanbee, on head. 1953. $16.00. (Courtesy Carolyn Powers)

Effanbee--21'' ''Dy-Dee'' This is the one used by the American Red Cross for teaching classes on handling babies. She is big and heavy. Molded hair, sleep eyes and a big mouth. Original clothes. Marks: EFFANBEE, on neck. EFFANBEE/DY-DEE BABY, on shoulders. $85.00. (Courtesy Phyllis Houston)

Effanbee--24'' ''Candy Walker'' Hard plastic, pin through, walker legs. Head turns. (Saucy Walker type). Arms are strung. Vinyl head with sleep blue eyes/lashes. Rooted hair. Original dress. Marks: Effanbee, on head. 1956. $20.00. (Courtesy Marie Ernst)

Effanbee--19½" "Alyssia-1958" Heavy hard plastic walker, head turns. Excellent quality stuffed vinyl head. Sleep blue eyes/lashes with slightly molded lids. Closed smile mouth. Rooted ponytail. Original red velvet dress/white trim. All fingers separate. Marks: Effanbee, on head. $75.00. (Courtesy Kathleen Flowers Council)

Effanbee--Shows close up of the head of the 1958 Alyssia doll. (Courtesy Kathleen Flowers Council)

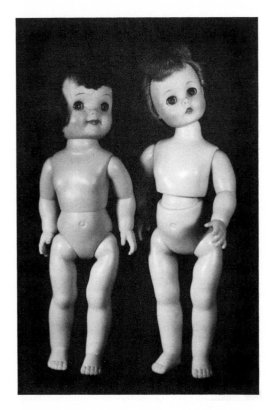

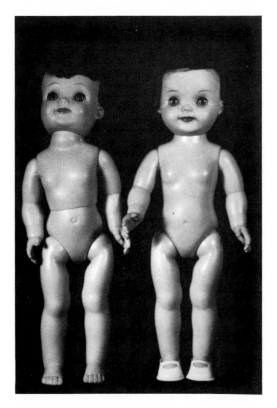

Effanbee--Shows the jointed waist Patsy Ann with an Alexander MaryBel to show difference of body construction. 1959. (Courtesy Phyllis Houston)

Effanbee--15" "Patsy Ann" Two versions of doll. Both are all vinyl, have same faces with blue sleep eyes, auburn rooted hair, freckles, closed mouth with slight smile. One has strung head that is fully posable and a jointed waist. Other is fully flanged and has non-jointed waist. Marks: EFFANBEE/PATSY ANN/(C) 1959, on neck of both dolls. $20.00. (Courtesy Phyllis Houston)

Effanbee--11½" "Black Pumpkin" Plastic and vinyl. Original. Marks: Effanbee/1966, on head. $12.00. (Courtesy Anita Pacey)

Effanbee--10" "Pumpkin Boy and Girl" Boy has freckles. Plastic and vinyl. Marks: Effanbee/1966, on heads. Boy $15.00. Girl $12.00. (Courtesy Anita Pacey)

Effanbee--11" "Pumpkin Bicentennial Doll" All vinyl with freckles. Dressed in red/white and blue. 1976. $15.00. (Courtesy Anita Pacey)

Effanbee--11" "Pumpkin Bicentennial Girl" All vinyl with sleep blue eyes. Dressed in red/white and blue. 1976. $15.00. (Courtesy Anita Pacey)

Effanbee--This group is the Grand Dames of
1975. The group includes the Mrs. Miniver.
$65.00 each. (Courtesy Anita Pacey)

Effanbee--18½'' ''Mrs. Miniver''
Multi stripe red with black trim.
Marks: Effanbee, on head.
(Courtesy Anita Pacey)

During 1974 the Effanbee Company introduced a "limited Edition Doll Club". Unfortuantely they started it with an already produced doll "Precious Baby" and costs $40.00 instead of creating a different doll that had never been on the market. Maybe as time goes by they will introduce a true Limited Edition doll. Information on the club can be gotten from: Effanbee Dept. L, 508 West 26th St., New York, N.Y. 10001

Effanbee--16½" "Patsy-1976" All vinyl with molded brown hair. Blue sleep eyes. Pink cotton dress with white organdy. Marks: Patsy/Limited Edition/1976, on head. Effanbee/"Patsy" /Limited Edition/1976, on back. Dress tagged also. $65.00. (Courtesy Phyllis Houston)

Effanbee--15" "Black Chipper Bride and Bridesmaid" 11" "Black Pumpkin Ring Boy and Flowergirl" 1975. It has been reported that Effanbee made 13 sets of the Black ring bearer and flowergirl for a dealer in Texas. The company will not comment on this. They were not offered to the general public. $250.00 set. (Courtesy Renie Culp)

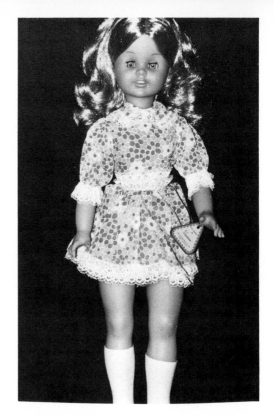

Eugene Dolls--19'' ''Baby Wendy'' Cloth with vinyl arms and legs. Hard plastic head. Sleep blue eyes/lashes and black shadow. Open mouth/tow upper teeth. Saran wig. 1952. Marks: APEX, on head. by Eugene Dolls, on tag. Original. $18.00. (Courtesy Marie Ernst)

Australia--25'' ''Vanessa'' All good quality vinyl with sleep blue eyes/lashes. Open.closed mouth. Polished nails and young teen breasts. Marks: None on doll. My name is/Vanessa/The House of Metti Pty. Ltd./Made in Australia, on tag. 1975. $32.00.

Australia--13'' ''Mon Cherie'' All good quality vinyl with sleep blue eyes/lashes. Closed mouth. Marks: None on doll. My name is Mon Cherie/Made in Australia, on tag. Metti, on original box. 1975. $16.00.

Australia--11¾'' ''Jenny, the Qantas Hostess'' Original dress which is the Qantas Airlines official colors. This is the Kenner Dusty Doll. Marks: 3632/189/G.M.F.G.I. Kenner Prod., on head. G.M.F.G.I. Kenner Prod./Cincinnati, Ohio 45202/Made in Hong Kong. Toltoys, on box. Jointed waist and lightly tanned. Solid vinyl arms and bending knees. $12.00.

Australia--This is the South Africa safari outfit for Jenny. Same as was sold for Dusty. $4.00.

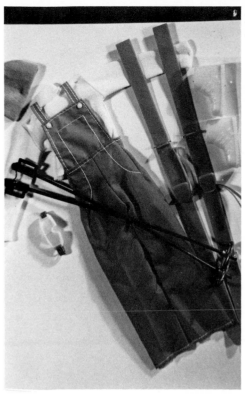

Australia--This Jenny outfit is Austria and same as sold in U.S.A. for Dusty. $4.00.

Australia--This is the Hawaiian outfit for Jenny with marked surf board. $8.00.

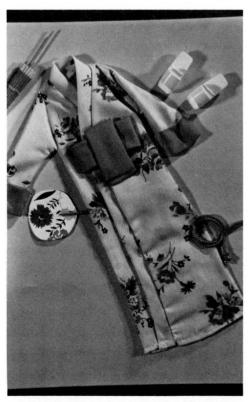

Australia--Shows the Qantas Hostess (Jenny) outfit: Japan. $8.00.

China--13" Oriental figures. Cloth over wire frames. Painted stockenette features. Floss hair. Attached to round wood bases. The manufacturer (Chinese-Taiwan) went out of business and these were available through the New York firm, Treasure Trove. 1976. $22.00 each.

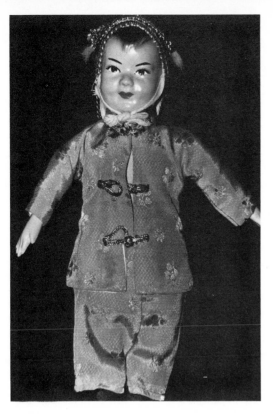

China--8½" Cloth with composition head, lower arms and feet. Character face. Original. $15.00. (Courtesy Mary Partridge)

England--15" Black Saucy Walker type with sleep brown eyes and open mouth with two upper teeth. Marks: Pedigree/International Aircraft Ltd/Merton, London/S.W.19 England. 1957. $75.00. (Courtesy Mrs. E. Bethscheider)

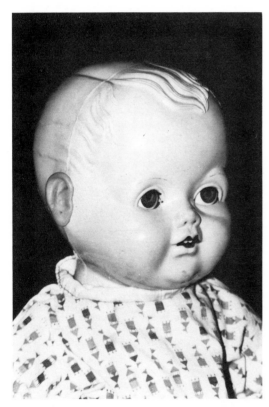

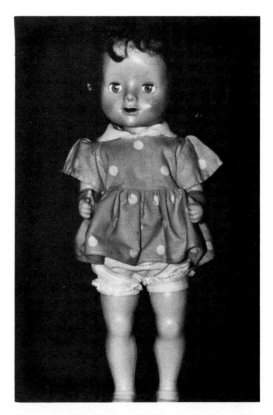

England--18" Cloth body with celluloid head. Very "heavy" molding around face. Sleep eyes. Open mouth with two upper teeth. Applied rubber ears. Molded hair. Painted bisque hands. Marks: PAT. NO. 535611/&/Foreign Patents. Made by Cascelloid, Ltd. and A.E. Pallet-Patented July 22, 1939. $45.00.(Courtesy Kimport Dolls)

England--12" "Martha" Hard plastic walker, head turns. Molded on shoes. Sleep blue eyes/lashes. Glued on mohair wig. "Wobbie" head. Left index finger is pointing, all right fingers are curled. Marks: Pedigree, on head. Made in England, on back. 1952. $16.00.

89

England--8" "H.R.H. Princess Anne" Head, legs & body one piece. Wig is glued on. This body was cut above waist and the two pieces jammed together and glued. Dress is white satin. $35.00. (Courtesy Phyllis Houston)

England--9" "French Gendarm" All foam over wire. Molded & painted clothes, hat etc. 1X, on collar and cap. Marks: BENDEE, on back. $5.00.

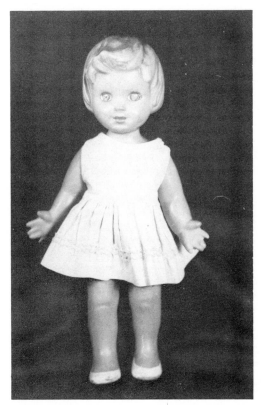

France--11½" Soft plastic one piece girl with molded hair and inset eyes. Marks: ⑤, on back. $8.00. (Courtesy Phyllis Houston)

France--20½" "GeGe" lady doll. Rigid plastic body and legs, vinyl head and arms, very pale blue sleep eyes, light blonde hair. Twist waist. Flat feet. Marks: GeGe/MC5, on neck. M5/Made in France, on shoulders. $15.00. (Courtesy Phyllis Houston)

France--12" "Chiffon" by the Princess Christina Company of France. Cloth with vinyl head and hands. Marks: None on doll. Dress tag: Made in France. 1974. $16.00. (Courtesy Helen Faford)

France--20½" "Clement & Cannelle" from Compagnie Du Jouet, France. Very pale high quality vinyl heads, arms and legs, stuffed bodies. Amber sleep eyes. Wigs are sewn to a cloth base and then sewn to heads. No additional color in cheeks or lips. She does have freckles. Dolls are unmarked except for cardboard tags on wrists. $30 each. (Courtesy Phyllis Houston)

France--Princess Christina: (International Toy Corp)* 23½" "Shane" Material*, sleep brown eyes with long lashes, rooted golden brown hair, open/closed mouth, soft shell complexion, all original. Marks: (R) ESMA/IN-DUSTRIA/ARGENTINA, on head. $40.00. (Courtesy Phyllis Houston)

Germany--Princess Christina: 18" "Tracy" with amber sleep eyes, rooted dark hair. Vinyl and plastic. Beautiful coloring and all original clothes. Marks:

W. Germany., on neck. $40.00. (Courtesy Phyllis Houston)

91

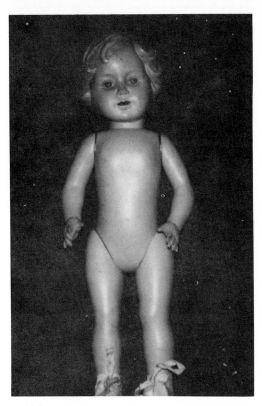

Germany--15" All rubber with painted blue eyes
and deeply molded hair. Marks: Steha, in
diamond/Made in/Western/Germany. 1950.
$8.00. (Courtesy Carolyn Powers)

Germany--12" "Corina" Black all vinyl baby
with vivid brown sleep eyes/lashes. Original.
Made by the Princess Christina Company of Germany. Marks: 36/ M ZAPF /Germany. $22.00.
(Courtesy Anita Pacey)

Germany--13" "Tommy" #9051. All pale vinyl
with brown sleep eyes/lashes, and rooted hair.
Original. Marks: 36/ M ZAPF /in Germany, on

back. Designed and made by the Princess
Christina Company of Germany. $22.00.
(Courtesy Anita Pacey)

Germany--16" "Sweet Sue" #9012. All pale vinyl
with brown sleep eyes/lashes. Rooted hair.
Original. Marks: Z /42, on head and 45, on

body. Made by the Princess Christina Company
of Germany. $22.00. (Courtesy Anita Pacey)

Germany--9½" "Limmer Puppe Um 1900"
Pressed mache type shoulder head. Vinyl legs and
boots. Original. Made in Germany. $35.00.
(Courtesy Connie Chase)

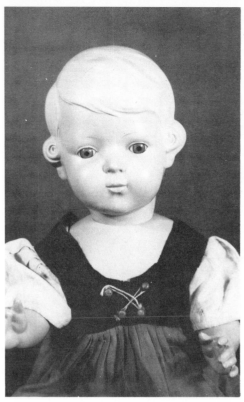

Germany--18" All celluloid with deeply molded
hair. Sleep blue eyes/no lashes. Original dress.
Marks: TURTLEMARK in diamond/45, on head
& back. Circa 1947. $65.00. (Courtesy Phyllis
Houston)

Germany--24" "Lise" Plastic body with vinyl
head and limbs. Cryer box in center back. Light
blue sleep eyes/lashes. Open/closed pouty mouth.
Very square jaw. Marks: 60, high on shoulders.
1966. $12.00. (Courtesy Phyllis Houston)

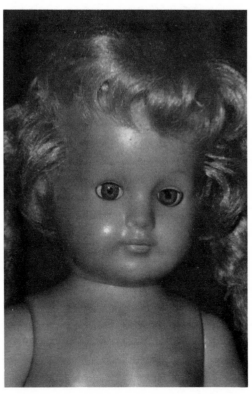

Germany--15" "Gret" All vinyl. Sleep blue eyes.
Marks: TURTLE/SCHILDKROT/GER-
MANY/40. 1963. Looks very much like Regal of
Canada's 1962 "Louise"-refer to series 11, page
96. $9.00. (Courtesy Marie Ernst)

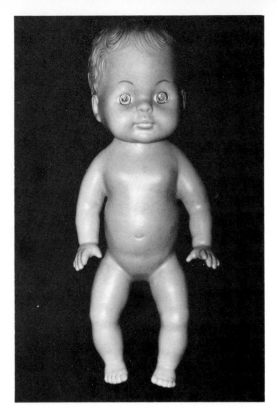

Hong Kong--18" "Mrs. Andrew's" and 3¼" "Quint Babies" All are a cheap plastic and all have inset blue eyes. Babies are jointed at shoulders only. Marks:  /Made in Hong Kong/218. $4.00. (Courtesy Marie Ernst)

Hong Kong--9" Rigid vinyl one piece body and softer vinyl head. Sunburned skin tones. Inset blue eyes. Marks: MADE IN/HONG KONG, on back. A Vogue copy. 1975. $1.00.

Hong Kong--6½" "Sad Song" One piece vinyl body and limbs. Vinyl head with very large painted eyes and tear. Sad closed mouth. Rooted hair. Feathered brows. Marks: PERFEC-TA/Made in Hong Kong, on head. British Design Appl./No. 923252/Made in Hong Kong, on base. 1965. $3.00.

Hong Kong--6" "Betsy Ross Pin Cushion" Half doll is all vinyl and jointed at neck and shoulders. Painted blue eyes. Marks: None on doll. JS NY 1975/MADE IN HONG KONG, on tag. $3.00.

94

Italy--18" "Athena" All plastic with vivid blue sleep eyes/lashes. Marks: Athena/40, on head. Athena/Piacenxa/40/P, on back. $65.00. (Courtesy Carolyn Powers)

Italy--9½" "Lenci Girl" Felt face, silky mohair wig. All original rayon and cotton clothes. Body and limbs of stuffed cotton with felt hands with stitched fingers. Felt shoes. Marks: Part of Lenci tag. $65.00. (Courtesy Phyllis Houston)

Italy--"Lenci": Mint in box! 15" girl with composition face, hollow felt body, felt legs & arms. Glued on blonde wig. Painted eyes are brown. Dress is a green rayon; green shoes and cape are made of felt. Green trimmed white underwear of cotton, with pants attached to slip. Marks: None on doll. LENCI/Made in Italy, on tag. No. on box is 371. $165.00. (Courtesy Phyllis Houston)

Italy--10" "Ciondolina" Green cloth body with rigid vinyl head. Plastic arms and legs. A "floppy" doll. Painted black eyes. Orange yarn hair. Marks: Sebino/Made in Italy. 1975. $6.00.

95

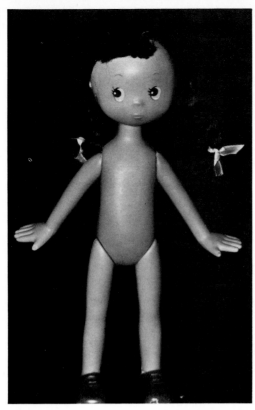

Italy--12½" "Melita" All dark pink plastic with red molded on shoes. Painted blue eyes & glued on hair. Marks: Sebino, on back. 1971. $1.00. (Courtesy Marie Ernst)

Italy--17" "Cosetta" (Many Kisses). Cloth with vinyl head and gauntlet hands. Painted blue eyes. Magnets in hands make her "kiss". Marks: MADE IN ITALY/SEBINO, on head. 1975. $8.00

Italy--14" "Dudu" All heavy vinyl with sleep eyes/lashes. Open mouth with retractable tongue. Press her back and the tongue comes out to lick her plastic sucker. Marks: 143/Sebino/Made in Italy, on head. 80, on back. 1975. $35.00.

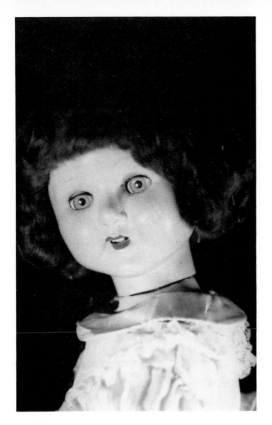

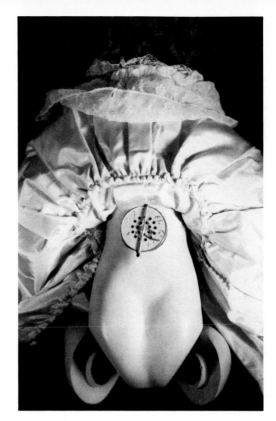

Italy-- 34'' All composition with long narrow body, blue sleep eyes. Open mouth/teeth & doll is strung. Cry box in back attached with hugh staple. Brown mohair wig is a replacement. Marks: None. $125.00. (Courtesy Phyllis Houston)

FURGA

Lombardy, situated in the center of Northern Italy, is a historic region, with lush vegetation and many water courses. It extends across the plane from the foothills of the majestic Alps as far as the calm, slow moving Po, Italy's longest river and is the hub of Italian economy and commerce. In fact, Lombardy can boast a higher number of cars, television sets, electrical household appliances, etc, per capita than any other region of Italy.

The capital of the region of Lombardy is Milan-the ancient Mediolanum-which is today a busy, cosmopolitan city, second only to Rome in population, and Italy's chief commercial and business center.

On the far Eastern boundary of this region, lies Canneto, which is in the province of Mantua and once was a part of the Duchy of Mantua, whose ancient fortress was the scene of historic meetings which took place between the Dukes of Mantua and Charles V of Spain, Philip II and other monarchs.

It was here in Canneto almost one hundred years ago (1870's) Luigi Furga Gorini, member of an old noble Mantuan family, founded the first Italian doll factory which is still today the largest of its kind in the country.

It is to his credit that, on the eve of the industrial age, he took the decision to keep up with the times and pioneer an industry which meant giving up the quiet, orderly life he was used to in order to become involved with all the problems, risks and tribulations of an industrialist.

Luigi Furga first conceived the idea of making dolls when he saw what papier mache carnival masks were being manufactured by a native of Canneto who had spent some time in Germany. From masks to dolls is a short jump, especially as the first dolls were made mainly of papier mache.

Furga, which started life as a small workshop and has now developed into a huge public (stock) company, still run by the descendants of the founder's family, has always kept the principles that dolls have value and fascination as well as excert a great influence on the minds of children. This is the secret of their continual success and ever-growing reputation.

During the 1870's, Furga's toy factory was mentioned in the old "Melzi" dictionary as a toy factory at Canneto and the modern encyclopedia "Treccani" states that the first doll in Italy came from Canneto. Furga has been awarded many certificates, gold medals and diplomas at shows, exhibitions and specialized fairs and has a reputation for first class quality.

Recently an article by Gerald Schurr appeared in Volume 160, No. 646, dated December 1965, of the well-known magazine, "The Connoisseur" in which he states that it has been decided to exhibit a Furga doll at the Paris "Musee des Arts Decoratifs", as it is an exquisite work of art.

Owing to the lack of space, it is impossible, to list all the publications, newspaper articles, magazines, etc. in every language which praise Furga dolls, even if the list were limited to cover just the past ten years.

The Chamber of Commerce at Mantua has given us the following official statistics: at the end of the last century there were 158 employees at Canneto in the manufacture of wax and papier mache dolls, whereas at the beginning by 1901 the number had increased to 234: 62 men and 172 women; about 1910 Furga began exporting to England, Brazil and other South American countries. By 1913 the export of dolls from Italy was almost entirely in the hands of Furga.

During a span of almost 100 years this firm has examined and applied all possible techniques known to the doll industry. They have followed, and often pioneered the way to, technological developments in both the industrial and fashion fields.

At first the dolls had papier mache limbs and wax heads, then stuffed rag bodies and wax or papier mache heads, at the beginning of this century the bodies were made of papier mache, the limbs of polished wood and the heads of china. Just after the first world war (1914-1918) a new source of supply had to be found as the biscuit china heads had previously been imported from Germany; Furga therefore built their own plant for the manufacture of the biscuit heads themselves.

All the dolls manufactured up till then had been either semi or completely jointed, with painted eyes, sleep glass eyes or set glass eyes, some with and some without talking devices, some fully dressed and others simply dressed in a petticoat.

The first dolls appeared on the market with stuffed bodies and "pastel" heads (a sort of ground papier mache mixed with koalin) and, in cases of the more expensive models, dolls with limbs and bodies in painted papier mache, papier mache heads and movable eyes which blinked, and wigs made of mohair wool set in ringlets; in the case of the luxury models, real human hair was used and the dolls were dressed in gorgeous dresses.

During this period the manufacture of the so-called 18th Century crinoline dolls was started. These dolls were wearing crinoline skirts decorated with lace, coquettish white wigs, saucy beauty spots on the cheek bone and a jaunty three-cornered hat.

Furga was the first, in Europe, to introduce a "plastic" sheet (made of calendered polyvinyl choride), electronically welded, especially designed for the "baby" type doll that took the place of the traditional rag body.

The system of attaching tufts of hair directly into the dolls head dates back to 1947. This process was carried out, at first, by hand. Furga had already brought out a special machine when the first "rooting machine" appeared on the market.

Furga uses a lot of polystyrene and the dolls limbs, body and heads are injection molded in two halves which are joined together and colored flesh pink, creole tan, brown or yellow. The dolls intended for Africa have bright scarlet protruding lips and wear raffia skirts; those going to the Far East have almond-shaped eyes, high cheek-bones and wear kimonos.

There are walking dolls, laughing dolls, crying dolls, drinking dolls, all in a fantastic kaleidescope of shapes, sizes and colors. There is even a Furga doll with a revolving head and bonnet with three faces.

The most modern dolls are made of plasticized polyvinyl chloride which is baked in a kiln in fixed or revolving molds; these dolls are soft like real babies. Then there are blown polyethylene dolls which have been sand blasted beforehand and then made opaque by adding a mixture of rubber materials, and the very latest dolls are made of foam resins, based on polyvinyl materials, polyurethane, etc.

At present Furga is divided into two industrial units, one at Canneto and the other at Remedello, in another province of Lombardy, and one of the characteristics of Furga is the manufacture of their own clothes and accessory items. Furga has their own box factory, workshops for manufacture of molds and equipment, machinery for working wood and shop areas to make their own accessories, such as eyes, vocal boxes, socks, shoes, and all the metal smallware and devices which are used for making the dolls moveable and flexible. They also have a spinning mill for making acrylic resins, a laundry and a weaving department.

The synthetic resins and chemicals are purchased as raw materials and in the factory they undergo mixing, coloring and, if neccessary, aging treatments and processes.

Sculptors and doll fashion designers have their own departments and a studio for fashion research, chemical laboratories, programming and scheduling departments, all employing teams of artists and technicians.

The Commercial and Administrative departments have offices in Milan, Italy's largest business center, and all this and the data processing department plus show rooms occupy six floors of one building.

The present work force employed is 1,150 plus the office staff and line managers but added to this number are the ones who work at home and the independent workers scattered all around and are employed in sewing exclusively for the doll industry, then the figure far exceeds 1,500. Daily production exceeds 20,000 pieces, including finished dolls and doll's dresses.

Furga has built their reputation as one of the foremost doll makers and their pride of the Italian industry by solidly keeping to their traditional methods and principles of more than a hundred years and are always looking for a new possibilities of expression.

Collector's have always appreciated the Furga dolls, not only the fantastically dressed ones but also the babies and children. It is interesting that ALL Furga doll seem to be highly collectable whereas some of the U.S. made dolls such as the Madame Alexanders, the babies seem to be overlooked and collectors seem to be most interested in the "well dressed" ones only.

All Furga dolls are marked both with the name "Furga" and some with the word "Italy".

Italy--17" "Dama Louise" Set green eyes/lashes. Large scalp part in front. Original. Marks: FURGA ITALY, on head and body. $12.00. (Courtesy Marie Ernst)

Italy--11" "Furina" Rigid plastic body, head and legs. Vinyl arms. Glued on brown wig. Pale blue sleep eyes. Cryer. Original clothes. Marks: None on doll. FURGA/MADE IN ITALY, on tag. 1955. $75.00.

Furga--17'' ''Candida'' 1968. Bride. $75.00.

Furga--17'' ''Ondina'' 1968. Dress is graduated orange with orange and yellow flowers in hat. $75.00.

Furga--17'' ''Katrina'' 1968. Dress is deep rose with lime green leaves. $75.00.

Furga--15'' ''Margherita'' 1969. Dress is pink check with white trim. $75.00.

Furga--15'' ''Paolina'' 1969. Dress is pale blue with white trim. $75.00.

Furga--18'' ''Sanny'' with white hair and ''Susan'' with red hair. 1969. $12.00.

Furga--15'' ''Annamaria'' Soft plastic. Cryer. Sleep blue eyes. 1969. $20.00.

Furga--15'' ''Tonia'' 1969. Deep rose with white trim. $75.00.

Furga--15'' ''Gloria'' 1969. Blue coat with white dress. $45.00.

Furga--19" "Pisanella" Talking and singing doll with interchangeable records in Italian, French, English, German, Dutch, Spanish and Swedish. Battery operated. 1969. $22.00.

Furga--19" "Nicoletta" Plastic and vinyl. Sleep blue eyes. With pacifier or bottle, her lips move and she gurgles. Battery operated. 1969. $12.00.

Furga--19" "Pia and Paolina" All vinyl. Blue sleep eyes. 1969. $12.00.

Furga--20" "Serenella" Battery operated. She laughs when tossed into the air. 1969. $18.00.

Furga--25" "Agostina Toc Toc" Press an ear to chest and the "heart" beats. 1969. $18.00.

Furga--25" "Cicciotto" Vinyl fat baby. Open mouth/nurser. 1969. $12.00.

Furga--19'' ''Arianna'' 1969.
''Claudina'' 1970. $18.00.

Furga--26'' ''Manuela'' Open
mouth nurser. Cries tears. 1969.
$14.00.

Furga--12'' ''Fiorella'' Plastic and
vinyl with blue sleep eyes. 1969.
$10.00.

Furga--13'' ''Tonina'' Plastic and
vinyl battery operated talker. Also
comes in boy version, ''Tino''.
1969. $16.00.

Furga--9'' ''Giacomina'' All
vinyl. Sleep blue eyes. The
open/closed mouth version is called ''Gelsomina''. 1969. $6.00.

Furga--24'' ''Mary'' Cloth with
gauntlet vinyl hands. Vinyl head.
There are 3 different Mary's.
Mary Sioux is dressed as an Indian. Mary Gambalunga in black
with red skirt and vest that has
playing cards painted on. This one
is Mary LaRossa. 1970. $20.00.

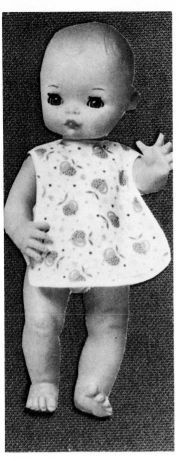

Furga--6½" "Gipi" Vinyl mini doll twin. Other is "Cipa" with dark hair. Both are girl dolls. 1969. $6.00.

Furga--13" "Brunello" All vinyl. Sleep blue eyes. Turned up left foot. 1969. $6.00.

Furga--16" "Dada" All vinyl. Open mouth/nurser. 1969. $8.00.

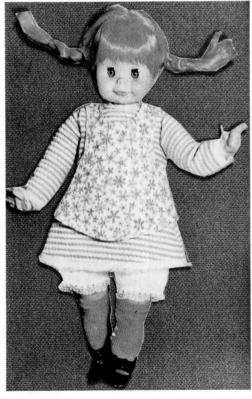

Furga--22" "Marianna" All soft filled body, arms and legs. Gauntlet vinyl hands, vinyl head. 1969. $18.00.

Furga--26" "Petronilla" Cloth body. Vinyl gauntlet hands, legs and head. Red rooted hair. Green eyes. Freckles. 1970 was called "Teresa" and came dressed in bluish grey dress with red/white checkered ribbon bow at neck. White hose and red shoes. 1969. $9.00.

Furga--15" "Marinella" Plastic and vinyl. Sleep blue eyes. 1969. $12.00.

Furga--18" "Musetta" Plastic and vinyl. 1969. $12.00.

Furga--Left to right. All 22½". "Barberina", "Biancamaria" and "Beatrice". 1969. $65.00 each.

Furga--15" "Gloria" Soft plastic. Sleep eyes. Cryer. 1969. $22.00.

Furga--Left to right. All 18". "Valeria", "Valen-tina" and "Veronica". 1969. $55.00 each.

Furga--18" "Paolina" 1970. $20.00.

Furga--17" "Angela" 1970. $20.00.

Furga--27½" "Orsola" Light brown eyes. With white hair dressed in navy blue/white. "Ofelia" dressed in tan & white coat with brown knee length boots and black hair. "Oriana" 1970. $18.00.

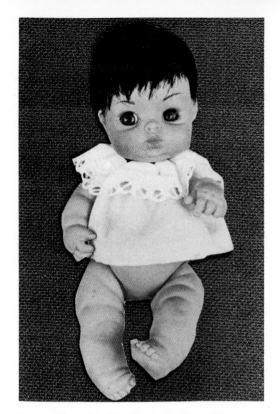

Furga--50'' Flat cloth doll. Girl is ''Cesarina'' and boy is ''Casimiro''. 1970. $4.00.

Furga--6'' ''Nana'' All vinyl. Sleep blue eyes. $4.00.

Furga--10½'' ''Flic'' All vinyl. Sleep blue eyes. 1970. $6.00.

Furga--10½'' ''Floc'' All vinyl. Sleep blue eyes. $6.00.

Furga--17'' ''Cosetta'' Battery operated walker. 1970. $16.00.

Furga--9½'' ''Pauline'' Walking doll. Battery operated. 1970. $6.00.

Furga--9½'' ''Nanette'' Plastic and vinyl walking doll. Battery operated. 1970. $6.00.

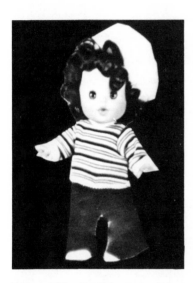

Furga--19'' ''Felicina'' Talking doll with 2 changable records. 1970. $12.00.

Furga--12'' ''Marcella'' All vinyl. Came in nine different outfits. 1970. $8.00.

Furga--16'' ''Doretta'' 1970. $6.00.

Furga--19'' ''Felicina'' Talking doll with 2 changable records. Bright red hair. 1970. $20.00.

Furga--14'' ''Carola'' All vinyl. Blue sleep eyes. 1970. $8.00.

Furga--19" "Bambina" Talker, lips move. Battery operated. Comes with two records. 1970. $25.00.

Furga--19" "Flavia" Battery operated talking doll. Comes with two records in English. 1970. $22.00.

Furga--17" "Irina" 1970. $50.00.

Furga--22" "Daniela" 1970. Aqua/white stripes. $65.00.

Furga--17" "Ilaria" 1970. Rose pink with white fir trim. $65.00.

Furga--27½" "Enrichetta" 1970. Rose with white fir on hat. $65.00.

Furga--27½" "Evelina" 1970. Blue with black trim. $65.00.

Furga--27½" "Eloisa" 1970. Blue with white trim. $65.00.

Furga--15" "Silvana" 1970. Beige with brown fir. $45.00.

Furga--15" "Sara" 1970. White with pink stripes & trim. $45.00.

Furga--22" "Desire" 1970. Aqua with white trim. $65.00.

Furga--18" "Chiara" 1970. White coat with brown trim. $18.00.

Furga--18" "Cecilia" 1970. Royal blue dress with white trim and hair. $18.00.

Furga--18" "Colomba" 1970. White dress, red hair and yellow boots & ribbon sash. $18.00.

Furga--17" "Agata" 1970. Red coat/white trim. Red/white stripped hose. $18.00.

Furga--19" "Mansueto" Vinyl with arms jointed to fully rotate. Very pale blue eyes. 1970. $22.00.

Furga--14" "Liliana" All vinyl. Came in 9 different outfits. 1970. $6.00.

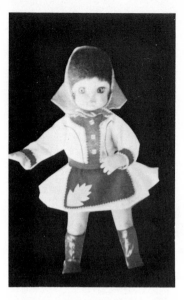

Furga--19'' "Martina" Same body construction as Mansueto. 1970. $20.00.

Furga--27½'' "Novellina" Battery operated talker. Tells stories. 1970. $25.00.

Furga--17'' "Ileana" 1970. Red/white checked dress. Red trim. $50.00.

Furga--20'' "Paolotta" 1970. $20.00.

Furga--22'' "Debora" 1970. Red and white. $65.00.

Furga--8½'' "Napoleone" All vinyl with inset eyes. 1973-74. $6.00.

Furga--18'' "Mia" 1973-74. $12.00.

Furga--18'' "Paola" Had extensive wardrobe. 1973-74. $12.00.

Furga--20'' ''Andrea'' Toss her in the air and she will laugh. 1973-1975. $9.00.

Furga--20'' ''Poldina'' Spank her and she will cry. 1973-75. $9.00.

Furga--8½'' ''Giuseppina'' All vinyl. Inset eyes. 1973-74. $4.00.

Furga--Left to right: 18'' ''Simonetta'', 18'' ''Eugenia'' & 18'' ''Elisabetta''. 1973-74. $55.00 each.

Furga--17" "Paola", "Peonia" and "Perea". All are same doll with different hair color. All vinyl. Marks: Furga/13801, on head. 1973-74. $18.00. (Courtesy Anita Pacey)

Furga--12" "Dama" with her hat on backwards because owner likes it that way. Mint. 1972. Blue sleep eyes, long pale blonde rooted hair. Scarlet velvet costume. $15.00. (Courtesy Phyllis Houston)

Furga--17" "Furga Ballerina" Has sleep eyes with long lashes and very long rooted red hair. Marks: Italy, on head. 1974. $22.00. (Courtesy Marie Ernst)

Furga--12" "Fiorelli" All vinyl with sleep blue eyes. Came as blonde and brunette and had various costumes. Marks: Furga/Italy, on head. 1974. $6.00. (Courtesy Anita Pacey)

Furga--15" "Facciatosta" Press stomach and eyes change as well as mouth. 1974-75. $4.00.

Furga--22" "Titina" Cloth body and legs. Polyfoam arms and head. Sleep brown eyes. 1975. $16.00.

Furga--20" "Tai-Lai" Eyes of the Far-East. 1975. $35.00.

Furga--18" "Pritti Millemosse" Can bend knees and ankles. Has jointed waist. Has extensive wardrobe and freckles across nose. 1975. $18.00.

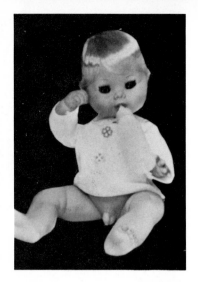

Furga--17" "Tomasino" Open mouth/nurser. 1973-74. Still available.

Furga--15" "Mimi" 1973. Pale blue and white checked. $55.00.

Furga--15" "Rosetta" 1973. All pink with pink feather cape. $55.00.

Furga--9" "Brunetta", the Summertime Queen. Green felt dress with green head band. 1975. Still available.

Furga--22½" "Le Damine" 1975. Rose with white trim. Still available.

Furga--18" "Pritti" with grow hair feature. jointed at waist. Straight legs. 1975. $12.00.

Furga--22" "Tata" Polyfoam. Sleep eyes. 1975. $10.00.

Furga--15" "Sabrina" 1975. Very pale blue with white trim. $55.00.

114

Furga--Left to right: 18'' ''Cecilia'', 18''
''Chiara'' and 18'' ''Corinna'' 1975. $55.00.

Furga--Left to right: 22½'' ''Valentina'', 22½''
''Veronica'' and 22½'' ''Vivana''. 1975. $55.00.

Furga--15'' ''Simona'' 1975. Gray
with trim of red & red/yellow
flowers. $55.00.

Furga--15'' ''Samanta'' 1975.
Red/green/white. $55.00.

Japan--4" Stone bisque of the 1930's. All original with mohair glued on wig. Jointed shoulders only. No wings. Marks: MADE IN/JAPAN, on back. $6.00. (Courtesy Phyllis Houston)

Japan--2" "Dolly Sisters" All celluloid with jointed shoulders only. Marks: Japan, on box and dolls. 1930's. $3.00 each. (Courtesy Anita Pacey)

Japan--8" "Love-Bug" All vinyl with large painted eyes. Closed smile mouth with one large molded tooth. All fingers & toes individually molded. Rooted hair. Marks: HEDAYA & CO. INC. 1966/JAPAN, on head. $2.00. (Courtesy Marie Ernst)

Japan--14" "Petta" Vinyl head with dublon-like limbs & cloth body. Almost round brown sleep eyes. Rooted hair. Open/closed mouth. Marks: 1973. $6.00. (Courtesy Phyllis Houston)

Japan--14'' ''Barbra Streisand'' Good quality vinyl and plastic. Jointed waist. Original. Large painted eyes. Marks: None. Dress tag: Same as ''Petta'' on next page. 1965. $55.00. (Courtesy Betty Tait)

New Zealand--23½'' Composition shoulder head on stuffed cloth body with ½ composition arms. Molded, painted hair. Painted brown eyes. Very crude composition. Marks: P.P. N.Z. $20.00. (Courtesy Phyllis Houston)

Norway--12'' ''Lupin'' All vinyl with sleep eyes/lashes and freckles. Original. Marks: None on doll. Grimstad Dukker/Grimstad, Norway, on tag. $22.00. (Courtesy Helen Faford)

Wales--7½'' ''Queen Elizabeth II'' Elaborately dressed in her long flowing train, blue ribbon and Garter & Cross. $35.00.

Wales--7½'' ''Lady Hamilton'' Lord Nelson's lady friend and ''Jane Seymore'' Plastic. Marks: None. Both designed by Odette Aiden. Removable clothes. Jointed shoulders only. Painted features. 1969. $35.00.

Wales--8½'' ''Prince of Wales'' as presented to the Welsh people at Caernavon Castle, North Wales in 1969. At this Investment he was created Prince of Wales. Before that he was Prince Charles. $45.00.

Wales--7½'' ''Mary, Queen of Scots'' Daughter of Henry VIII & half sister to Elizabeth the 1st. Was beheaded in the Tower of London. Removable clothes. Plastic with painted features. Jointed shoulders only. Designed by Odette Aiden. 1969. $35.00.

Wales--7½'' ''Anne Boleyn'' Beheaded so Henry VIII could re-marry. Plastic. Removable clothes. Jointed shoulders only. Painted features. Marks: None. Designed by Odette Aiden. 1969. $35.00.

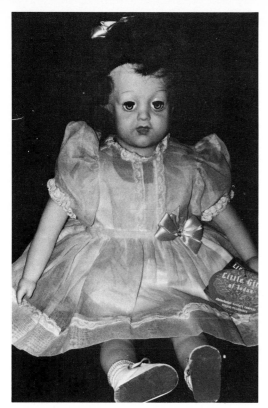

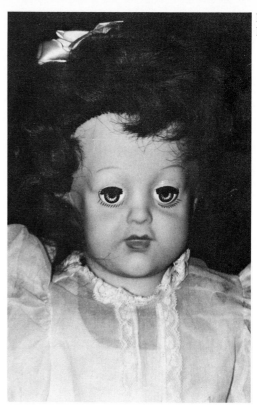

Fleischaker Novelty--23" "Little Girl of Today" Cloth body with stuffed early vinyl head and limbs. Character face with sleep blue eyes. Rooted human hair. Head is made in one piece on a shoulder plate and this is attached to the cloth body. Marks: Fleischaker Novelty, across front shoulder plate. Original. 1949-1951. (Author). $125.00.

This is a close-up of the face of the Girl of Today doll.

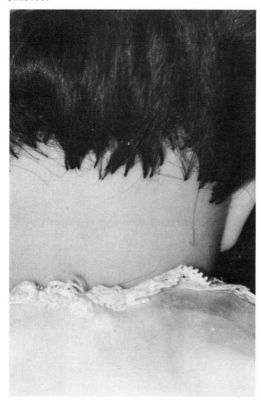

Shows the way the hair is hand rooted in the Girl of Today doll.

Freundlich, Ralph--11" "Baby Sandy" All composition with molded hair and sleep eyes. Open mouth with two upper teeth. All original with pin. Represents child star Sandy Henville. 1936. $95.00. (Courtesy Jay Minter)

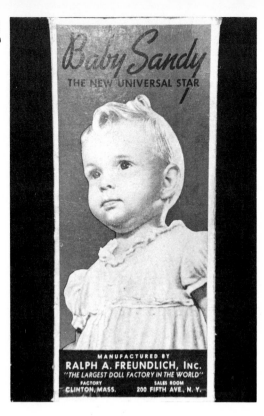

Freundlich, Ralph--Shows the original box top for the Baby Sandy.

Fun World--8½'' Action figures, each with portrait face. Marks: Hong Kong, on head. Left to right: Abe Lincoln, Uncle Sam and George Washington. 1975-76. $8.00 each.

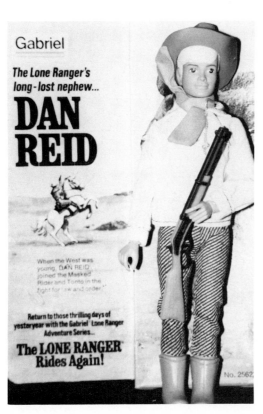

Gabriel--8" "Dan Reid" the Lone Ranger's long-lost nephew. Fully jointed action figure. Molded light blonde hair. Painted blue eyes. Marks: 1975 LONE RANGER/tel/ Inc./MADE IN HONG KONG/FOR GABRIEL IND. INC., on lower back. $8.00.

Gabriel--8½" "Timmy" Full jointed action figure. Lassie has full joints and pup is molded in one piece. Excellent detail and painting on dogs. Marks: 1975 Gabriel Industries Inc./Made in Hong Kong, on Timmy. Lassie: 1976 Gabriel Ind. Inc./Hagerstown, Md/1976 Lassie TV Inc/Made in Hong Kong, inside left leg. $8.00.

121

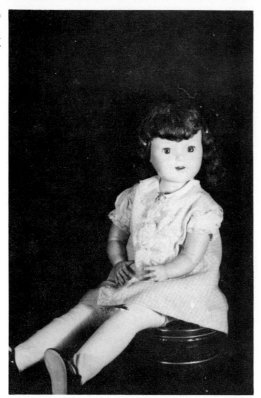

Halco--29" "Miss Fluffee" hard plastic shoulder head with hard plastic shoulder plate. Stuffed cloth body with sewn on stuffed latex legs and early stuffed vinyl arms. Sleep eyes/lashes. Glued on wig. Clothe not original. Open mouth with teeth and tongue. Made by J. Halpern Co. Pittsburg, Pa. (Halco) in 1951. Marks: None. $20.00. (Courtesy Phyllis Houston)

Hall Syndicate--15" "Margaret" Cloth with vinyl head. Painted on glasses. Friend to Dennis the Menace. Marks: 1968/HALL SYNDICATE INC. $16.00. (Courtesy Connie Chase)

Hallmark--12" "Sas-parilla, the Witch" All felt and velour. $4.00. (Courtesy Nancy Lucas)

Hallmark--13" "Betsy Clark" Cloth with vinyl head and gauntlet hands. Painted features. Has sad face. Original removable clothes. Made by Knickerbacher Toy Co. for Hallmark Cards, Inc. Marks: 1975 Hallmark Cards, Inc./K.T.C./Made in Tiawan. The original/Betsy Clark/Doll/Copyright 1975/Hallmark Cards, on tag. Also came in 9" size. Still available.

Hallmark--3" "Pin Cushion" All felt hamburger and olive. I had to show you this pin cushion to dramatize the changes of the times! Tag: HALLMARK/CARDS INC./MADE IN KOREA/200 DT 806-2/PIN CUSHION. $2.00.

Hallmark--6" "Snow Man" All stuffed terri cloth. Plastic eyes. Marks: None on doll. HALLMARK/CARDS INC/MADE IN TAIWAN/200XDT 46-5/DOLL TOY, on tag. $2.00.

Hallmark--4½" "Rain Deer" All good quality stuffed terrie cloth & felt. All four legs sewn together. Marks: None on doll. HALLMARK/CARDS INC/ MADE IN TAIWAN/200XDT 48-5/DOLL TOY, on tag. $2.00.

Hallmark--6" "Doll Toy" Stuffed cotton and felt. Plastic eyes. Orange mohair stitched on hair. Marks: None on doll. HALLMARK/CARDS INC./ STOCK NO. 200XDT 49-2/DOLL TOY, on tag. $2.00.

Hallmark--9" "Bean Bag Rabbit" All white flannel with yarn tail and hair. Pink cotton ears and ribbon. Body only is "bean" stuffed. Marks:HALLMARK/CARDS INC./MADE IN TAIWAN/25008119-1 BEAN BAG, on tag. $2.00.

Hallmark--6" "Henny", "Beloved Belindy" & "Uncle Clem" Marks: None on doll. HALLMARK/CARDS INC/MADE IN TAIWAN/each name/1974 THE BOBBS -MERRILL CO. INC, on tag. Still available in some areas. $3.00 each.

Hallmark--4½" "Raggedy Ann" All cloth. Orange yarn hair. Marks: RAGGEDY ANN DOLL/KNICKERBACHER TOY CO INC/MADE IN TAIWAN/REPUBLIC OF CHINA/HALLMARK CARDS INC./KANSAS CITY, MO. 64141, on tag. 1972. $3.00.

Hallmark--6" "Little Lulu" All cloth. Brown yarn hair and non-removable red dress. Marks: Hallmark Cards Inc. Western Publishing Co. Little Lulu Doll Toy, on tag. $3.00. (Courtesy Nancy Lucas)

Hallmark--7" "Victor Vulture" All felt with plastic eyes. $4.00. (Courtesy Nancy Lucas)

Hallmark--6" "Tiny Tim" Dark red yarn hair and freckles. On original card for gift trim. $2.00. (Courtesy Nancy Lucas)

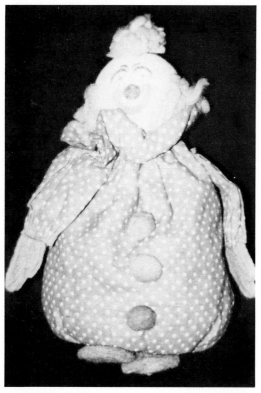

Hallmark--6" "Bean Bag Clown" Bean bag body of cloth with felt hands and feet. Orange yarn hair. Stuffed stockenette head. $2.00. (Courtesy Nancy Lucas)

Hallmark--10" "Spider" hand puppet. All black velvet-velour. Eyes painted on. Marks: Hand puppet, on tag. $4.00. (Courtesy Nancy Lucas)

Hartland--8" "Peter Brown" as Johnny McKay of the Lawman TV show of 1958. Very good quality plastic figure that is jointed at shoulders only. From a Warner Brothers Production. Marks: Hartland/Plastics, Inc., inside arm. Also made by Hartland: Matt Dillon/James Arness/Gunsmoke, John Lupton/Tom Jeffords/Broken Arrow, Gail Davis of the Annie Oakley Show, Hugh O'Brien/Wyatt Earp, DaleRobertson/Jim Hardie/Wells Fargo, Pat Conway/Clay Hollister/Tomestone Territory, Wayde Preston/Capt. Chris Colt of Colt 45, James Garner as Bret Maverick, Richard Boone as Paladin, John Payne/Vint Bonner/The Restless Gun, Clint Walker as Cheyenne, Ward Bond/Major Seth Adams/Wagon Train, Chief Thunderbird with horse Northwind, Robert E. Lee & horse Traveler, Gen. Custer & horse Buggler, Brave Eagle & horse White Cloud, Gen. George Washington & horse Ajax, Lone Ranger and Silver, Tonto and Scout, Jim Bowie & horse Blaze, Sgt. Preston of the Yukon & horse, Mickey Mantle, Ted Williams, Stan Musial, Henry Aaron, Ed Mathews, George "Babe" Ruth, Roy Rogers & Trigger, Dale Evans & horse Buttercup, Cochise with pinto & Buffalo Bill with horse. $16.00.

Hasbro--11½" Black early "G.I. Joe". Full action figure. Original. Marks: G.I. Joe TM/ Copyright 1964/ by Hasbro/Patent Pending/Made in U.S.A. $10.00. (Courtesy Betty Kirtley)

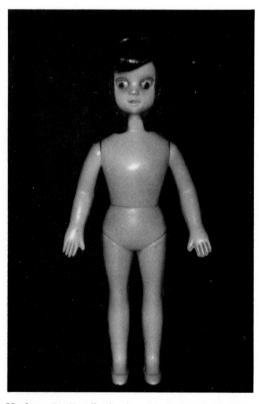

Hasbro--5¼" All plastic with shoulders jointed only. Molded brown hair. Painted eyes. Molded on shoes and panties. Marks: MADE IN USA/1968 Hasbro. $2.00. (Courtesy Virginia Jones)

This original set of G.I. Joes are marked: G.I. Joe Copyright 1964 by/Hasbro/Patent Pending/Made in U.S.A. There are no scar marks on faces. Top: Australian. Left: American. Kneeling left lower: Japanese. Center with headphones: English. Next: German and then Russian. Photo by LeRoy Seeley of Foshaug Studios. $18.00 each. (Courtesy Renie Culp)

Hasbro--12'' ''G.I. Joe'' dressed in special released outfit of an English Guard. $20.00. Courtesy Connie Chase.

Hasbro--8½'' ''Charlie's Angels'' Kelly (Jaclyn Smith) marked: 1862, on head. Sabrina (Kate Jackson) marked: 1861, on head. Jill (Farrah Fawcett Majors) marked: 1860, on head. Upper backs are marked: 1977/Spelling-Goldberg/Productions/All Rights/Reserved/Made in Hong Kong. Lower backs are marked: Hasbro/Pat. 3740894. Clothes are tagged: 1977 Hasbro/Made in Hong Kong. Still available except Jill. Jill $8.00.

HOLLYWOOD DOLL MANUFACTURING COMPANY.

The founder of Hollywood Dolls was Domenick Ippolite and he put more dolls on the market in 15 years than most manufacturers do in a life time. Hollywood dolls are well marked and came in painted bisque, composition and hard plastics. Unfortunately, this series of dolls must have original tag/box to know who they are.

Hollywood Dolls--6½'' ''Nun'' Sleep black eyes and legs are painted black. All plastic. Original. $8.00. (Courtesy Kathleen Flowers Council)

Hollywood Dolls--8'' ''Valentine'' Mid 1940's. All composition. Fully jointed. Molded on shoes/socks. Marks: HOLLYWOOD DOLL, on back. $10.00. (Courtesy Frances Anicello)

Hollywood Dolls--8'' ''Graduation Series'' Mid-40's. All composition with one piece head and body. Stapled on clothes. Molded shoes/socks. White dress/gold trim. $10.00. (Courtesy Mary Partridge)

Hollywood Dolls--5½'' All hard plastic girl, fully jointed with painted eyes. Original dress. Molded hair under removable wig. $8.00. (Courtesy Phyllis Houston)

Hollywood Dolls--4½" "Hollywood Baby" Original Bunny suit. Fully jointed and has sleep blue eyes. Marks: Hollywood Doll, around star, on back. $8.00. (Courtesy Kathleen Flowers Council)

Hollywood Dolls--Shows the body construction of the 4½" size baby. (Courtesy Kathleen Flowers Council)

HORSMAN DOLL COMPANY, INC.

The E.I. Horsman first began in 1865. Mr. Horsman was a member of an old established Germany toy making family and to start his business in the U.S.A., imported bodies and heads of bisque and put them together, here in the U.S.A.

By 1910, the Horsman Company was making many dolls of their own, including the Campbell Kids and many fine composition dolls. During the 1920's and 1930's, the Horsman Patsy type was called Dorothy and Sally. Later in the 1930's, their Shirley Temple type was called Shirley and wore a button pin. One of the most unique and original designers of Horsman dolls over the past 20 years has been a lady named Irene Szor. She sculptures the main design to be rendered by other artists and has made many, completely, of her own, which include: Mary Poppins, the Princess Line, Tuffy, Lil Charmer, Jackie (called Jacqueline Kennedy by collectors) and such characters as Gloria Jean, Hansel and Gretel, Baby Precious and last years model of The Blue Bird (Elizabeth Taylor).

Horsman Dolls in composition early vinyl and in the hard plastics are extremely fine quality dolls and very worthy to be in a collection.

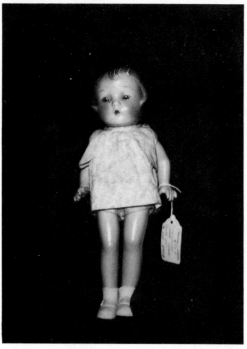

Horsman--10" "Babs" 1931. (Also came in 12" size) All composition with tin blue sleep eyes. 1934. Clothes made and designed by Mollye Goldman during the early 1930's. This doll is not original. $45.00. (Photo courtesy Carolyn Powers)

Horsman--16" "Jeanne" Cloth body with composition head and limbs. Small closed mouth, sleep tin eyes and molded topknot hair. Marks: Jeanne/Horsman, on head. 1937. $65.00. (Courtesy Gloria Harris)

Horsman--36" "Linda" Plastic and vinyl with long rooted hair. Sleep eyes/lashes. Marks: Horsman/1959. $85.00. (Courtesy Anita Pacey)

Horsman--19" "Sherry" Cloth body and rest vinyl. Green sleep eyes/lashes. Red rooted hair and open/closed mouth. Toddler legs. Marks: 2715/27 EYE/Horsman Dolls Inc./1967. $18.00.

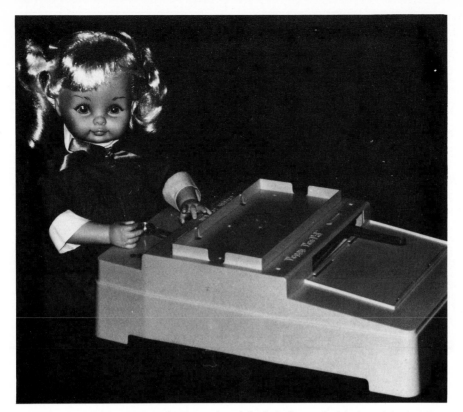

Horsman--18'' ''Peggy Pen Pal'' shown in original clothes and with the original writing desk. She has extra joints at the waist and elbows. Marks: 27/Horsman Dolls/1970. $12.00 complete. $5.00 doll only. (Courtesy Anita Pacey)

Horsman--These are original 17'' and 12'' ''Poor Pitiful Pearls'' made by Horsman in 1963. All original. It must be noted that Horsman re-issued this very same doll, with same mold marks, for the 1976 market. Marks: 1963/Wm. Steig/Horsman Dolls Inc., on head. $16.00. (Courtesy Mandeville-Barkel Collection)

Horsman--11'' ''Teensie Tot'' Plastic body and legs with vinyl head and arms. Sleep black eyes to side. Original. Marks: Horsman, on head. 1973. $6.00. (Courtesy Anita Pacey)

Horsman--6½'' ''Mini Thirstee'' baby. Sleep eyes. Open mouth/nurser. All vinyl. This doll also used with very long hair for the ''Zodiac baby''. Marks: FY1, on head. 1968-1973. $6.00. (Courtesy Phyllis Houston)

Horsman--10'' ''Beany'' Bean bag type filled cloth body, legs and upper arms. Vinyl head and hands. Rooted white hair and large painted blue eyes. Marks: Horsman Dolls Inc., on head. 1975. $4.00. (Courtesy Joan Amundsen)

Horsman--12½'' ''Pudgy'' All vinyl with very large painted eyes. Shoes are part of doll. Marks: HORSMAN DOLLS/1974. $6.00. (Courtesy Marie Ernst)

Horsman--14'' ''Sweet Memory'' Cloth with white vinyl gauntlet hands and white vinyl head. Long rooted hair. Sleep blue eyes/lashes. Open/closed mouth. Advertised as having ''bisque like vinyl''. Marks: HORSMAN DOLLS, INC.1975, on head. 1976. $8.00.

Horsman--11-3/4" "Elizabeth Taylor" Plastic with vinyl arms & head. Rooted dark brown hair. Large painted eyes with a light lavender wash over the eyes. Med. heel feet. Designed by Irene Szor. Dressed as "Light" from The Blue Bird. Marks: h, on head. 1976. $12.00.

Horsman--Elizabeth Taylor box. Doll comes dressed as Maternal Love and has been re-dressed as Light.

Hungerford--16" "Hungerford Baby Rosie Posie" All vinyl. Smile mouth with small nurser hole. Sleep eyes and molded hair with pointed topknot. Marks: Hungerford, on head. 1954. $22.00. (Courtesy Virginia Jones)

ICE CAPADE DOLLS

The costume department of the Ice Capades, long before each show, painstakingly dresses dolls. They have been doing this for over 20 years and it has been a guide to outfitting the entire cast. This process eliminates expensive mistakes. Mistakes can be costly as the most expensive items for each show is the elaborate costumes.

There are 125 workers in the costume department of Ice Capades and is a year round job. It is the designer for the show's costumes that make these mini ones and the costumes are in scale with the doll. They are sewn by hand, showing every bead, plastic mirror and sequin.

The dolls are taken on the road with the show's advance publicists amd make television appearances, are written up in the press and once in awhile are on display.

The designer and Director of Costumes finds these dolls a great time saver for colors and fabrics are tested as they must be light weight so the skater will not be hindered in skating. Spills do happen once in awhile, so fabrics must be waterproofed and the costumes must also be very durable.

The dolls are used in every department of the Ice Capades, the seamstresses use them for visual patterns, the set designers and technicians use them to coordinate the blending of colors, design and lighting. The dolls must be as perfect as the end result, the show on ice, itself. One mistake can be unbelievably expensive and one misjudgment in design can destroy the entire budget. The general cost for one years costumes comes close to a million dollars, with some of the "star" costumes costing close to $3,000 each.

The dolls are insured for $500.00 each and at the end of each year's tour the doll skaters are returned to the California studio where they are placed on display. Some have been sold and are now on the collector's market.

Six dolls are shown, along with descriptions & dates. These are now in the private collection of the author. It must be noted that over the years various dolls have been used. For a long time it was the Cissy by Alexander. The clothes are sewn on & non-removable.

Idenity of costumes courtesy of Ice Capades' costume shop manager, Mr. Armin Geltenpoth.

Ice Capades--17" Indian from "Rose Marie" 1949-1950. This is an all hard plastic Binnie Walker (face later to be Cissy). Walker, head turns and she has flat feet. Costume is of real leather with felt fringe. $185.00.

Ice Capades--20" "My Fair Lady" 1961-1962 season. This is the Cissy doll by Alexander with jointed knees and one piece vinyl arms. Outfit is royal blue and white with a great many sequins. The head piece is a large hat attached to a black sequin wig. $185.00.

Ice Capades--20" "Show Boat" This is a Cissy by Alexander with jointed knees and one piece vinyl arms. Her gown is white with pink ruffled ribbon and white sequin bodice. The head dress is feathers and very elaborate. She has matching rhinestone and sequin necklace. $185.00

Ica Capades--20" "Cole Porter" 1963. This is a Cissy by Alexander with jointed knees and one piece vinyl arms. Gown is redish rose velvet with rhinestone trim at bodice top. She has real fur trim around the hem line. $185.00.

Ice Capades--24" "Zodiac" number of 1968. The top is royal blue with silver sequins, as is the head dress. The streamers attached to top and arms are a silver foil. The basic body suit is flesh colored and the pantie part is sequined with attached blue cording. The doll is plastic and vinyl. Marks: 4373/K/1961, on the head. Made by Kaysam Doll, a part of Jolly Doll Company. $185.00.

Ice Capades--20" "Gypsy" number 1972. The body suit is flesh colored and black with black wig and multi colored scarf, with gold coin trim, coin necklace and coins attached to the leather boots. The skirt is multi colored and is detachable and held with velour strips. This doll is also by Kaysam (Jolly Toys). Marks: 4272/K/1961. $185.00.

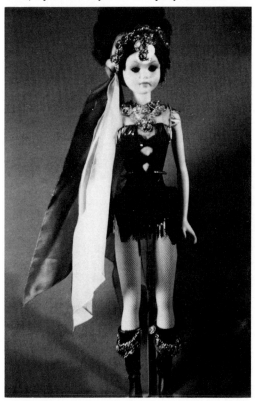

Ice Capades--This shows the Gypsy doll with her skirt removed. This particular outfit is just plain "fantasstic". The skirt has a sewn in label reading "Ice Capades", the others do not.

IDEAL TOY CORP.

Morris Michtom, in 1902, formed the Ideal Toy and Novelty Company to produce his Teddy Bear. By 1915, the company was well established and led the industry by the use of sleep eyes in composition dolls. In the early 1930's Ideal, now in the hands of the founders son, Benjamin F. Michtom, worked out an arrangement with Mollye Goldman and began making the Shirley Temple doll with Mollye making and designing all the clothes for the doll. The Shirley Temple doll is desirable for a collection but the most desirable doll, to todays collectors, would be the Ideal Judy Garland as Dorothy of the Wizard of Oz.

Ideal--18" "Peggy" 1931. Composition and cloth girl in all original costume. Very short arms. Straight composition legs. Stuffed cloth body. Tin sleep eyes, glued on wig. Marks: IDEAL TOY. $45.00. (Courtesy Phyllis Houston)

Ideal--12½" "Fannie Brice" commedienne of radio and stage. This doll represents the character, Baby Snooks. Flexy wire with composition hands, head and feet. 1939. $125.00. (Courtesy Jay Minter)

Ideal--13" "Mortimer Snerd" Flexy wire doll with composition head, hands and feet. This Edgar Bergen's character was a dummie but his mouth is un-movable in this doll. 1939. $95.00. (Courtesy Jay Minter)

Ideal--15" "Ginger" 1939. All composition with open mouth, brown sleep eyes with eyeshadow. Peach taffeta dress that buttons down the back. Marks: ⊗ , on head and Shirley Temple slightly rubbed out on back. $45.00. (Courtesy Marie Ernst)

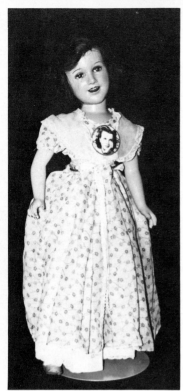

Ideal--This is a group of originally dressed Deanna Durbin dolls. 1939-1841. All composition with brown human hair wigs. Marks: Deanna Durbin/Ideal Doll. Top row: The first two are both 21'' and the last one is 27'' tall. Lower left is 21'' Ideal's Judy Garland Teen Star. All original and looks near to the Deanna Durbin. The eyes are slightly narrower and the mouth not as smiling. Marks: Ideal Doll/Made in USA, on head and Ideal Doll/backwards 21, on body. The doll on the right is Gulliver from ''Gulliver's Travels'', using the Deanna Durbin doll. Black mohair wig and brown sleep eyes. Original. Marks: Deanna Durbin (partially blacked out)/Ideal Doll, on head. $145.00 and up. (All dolls courtesy Mandeville-Barkel Collection except top left, which is courtesy Jay Minter)

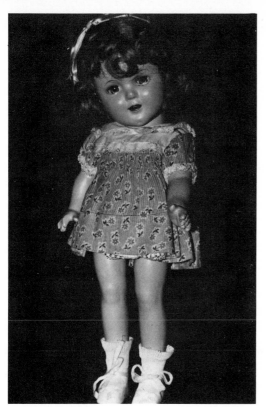

Ideal--13" "Marilyn Knowlden" (most known movie "Imitation of Life"). She was in a few pictures and expected to be a big star but this did not happen. All composition, open mouth with six teeth. Blue sleep eyes/lashes. Black eyeshadow and red mohair wig. Large dimple in chin. Original flowered dress from the movie. Marks: U.S.A./13, on back. Ideal Doll/Made in U.S.A., on head. 1935-1936. $95.00.

Ideal--18" "Shirley Temple" in Bluebird costume (from the movie of the same name). All composition. Marks: Shirley Temple, on head. U.S.A./Shirley Temple/18, on body. 1941. $200.00. (Courtesy Meisinger Collection)

Ideal--This shows three original dresses for the Ideal Toni dolls. 1949-1950. $28.00. (Courtesy Mandeville-Barkel Collection)

Ideal--21" "Toni" All hard plastic walker with glued on nylon wig. All original. Marks: Ideal Doll/P-93, on body. Genuine/Toni Doll, etc., on tag. 1950-1953. $45.00. (Courtesy Mandeville-Barkel Collection)

Ideal--17" "Posie" with original box. Hard plastic with jointed knees. Walker. Vinyl head with sleep blue eyes/lashes. Marks: Ideal Doll/VP-17, on head. 1954. $20.00. (Courtesy Anita Pacey)

Ideal--16" "Princess Mary" Hard plastic with vinyl head. Pin hipped walker, head turns. Marks: Ideal Doll/V-91, on head. Ideal Doll/16, on back. Original, but shoes are replaced. 1954. $25.00. (Courtesy Virginia Jones)

Ideal--20" "Honeysuckle" One piece stuffed vinyl body and limbs. Vinyl head with rooted hair, sleep blue eyes/lashes. Open/closed mouth. 1955. Marks: Ideal Doll, on head. $20.00. (Courtesy Anita Pacey)

Ideal--Shows the 20" "Honeysuckle" in her original box. (Courtesy Anita Pacey)

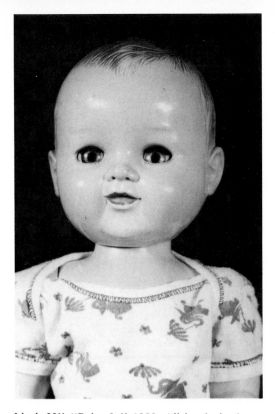

Ideal--22" "Baby Jo" 1955. All hard plastic on Saucy Walker type body with non-bending knees. Individual fingers. Breather with hole in nostrils. Pale blue sleep eyes and molded hair. Marks: Ideal Doll/Made in USA/22, on head. $18.00. (Courtesy Phyllis Houston)

Ideal--7½" "Lindy" All hard plastic. Sleep grey eyes. One piece body and head. Curved legs. Molded lashes. Possibly original dress. 1956. Marks: None. $3.00. (Courtesy Phyllis Houston)

Ideal--23" "Bonnie Walker" Hard plastic walker with pins through hips. Excellent coloring. Open mouth with four upper teeth. Blue flirty sleep eyes/lashes. Saran hair glued on. Marks: IDEAL DOLL/W-25, on head. IDEAL DOLL, on body. 1956. $28.00. - $22.00. (Courtesy Kimport Dolls)

Ideal--18" "Cousin Sue" 1957. Cloth body with vinyl head and limbs. Sleep blue/lashes. Open/closed mouth with upper teeth. Cute expression. Not original clothes. Marks: None, except on tag. $16.00. (Courtesy Phyllis Houston)

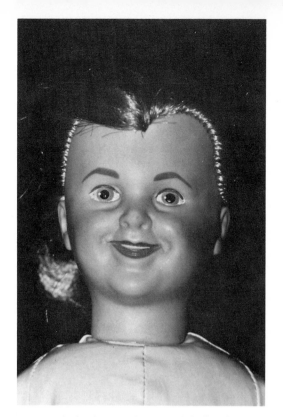

Ideal--13½" "Unknown Personality" Vinyl head and ½ arms. Spread fingers. Oilcloth body. Rooted hair with painted features. Open/closed mouth. Marks: None. $65.00.

Ideal--Shows a close up of the head.

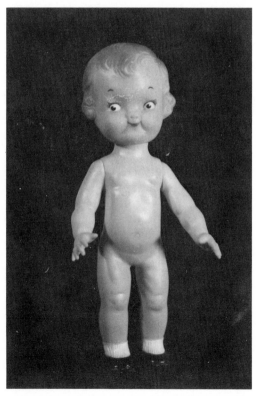

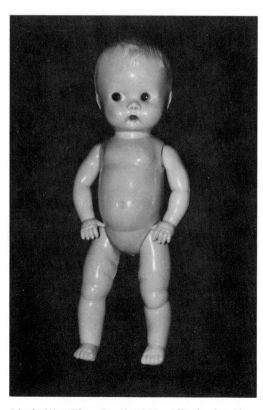

Ideal--8" "Campbell Kid" Jointed shoulders and head swivels. Painted on shoes and socks. All very good quality vinyl. hair is molded and eyes are painted. Marks: CAMPBELL KID/MADE BY/IDEAL TOY CORP. (No date shown). $8.00. (Courtesy Phyllis Houston)

Ideal--8" "Tiny Boy" 1960. All plastic. Sleep blue eyes to side. Molded hair. One piece head & body. Marks: IDEAL, in oval/PAT. PEND. $3.00. (Courtesy Marie Ernst)

Ideal--Two foot long plastic car that holds Jed, Jethro, Elly May, Granny and Duke from the T.V. show the "Beverly Hillbillies". Marks: Filmways T.V. Productions Inc./ 1963 Ideal Toy Corp., on box. $18.00. (Courtesy Anita Pacey)

Ideal--8½" "Dracky, Mini Monster" Plastic with vinyl arms and head. Original. Marks: 1965/Ideal Toy Corp/m-8½, on head. Made in Japan, on back. This set also included Vampy and Wolfy. $9.00.

Ideal--8½" "Franky, Mini Monster" Plastic with vinyl arms and head. Original. Marks: 1965/Ideal Toy Corp./M-8½, on head. Made in Japan, on back.

Ideal--30" "Betty Big Girl" Plastic with vinyl arms and head. Walker, head turns. Talker in back. Battery operated. Sleep light green eyes/lashes. Open/closed mouth with molded teeth. Marks: 1968/Ideal Toy Corp/HD-31-H-127, on head. 1969/Ideal Toy Corp./HB-32, on back. $85.00.

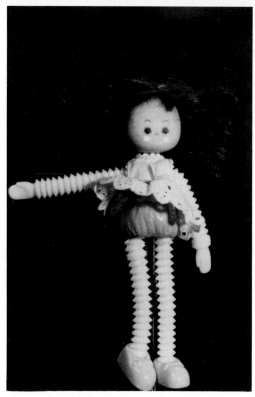

Ideal--7'' Plastic with vinyl head. Rooted hair and painted features. Original dress. Marks: 1972/IDEAL, in oval/H-202. $3.00. (Courtesy Phyllis Houston)

Ideal--22'' ''Baby Crissy'' Has pull string, grow hair feature. All vinyl and comes in black and white. Marks: 1972/Ideal Toy Corp/2 M-5511/B, on back. $16.00. (Courtesy Anita Pacey)

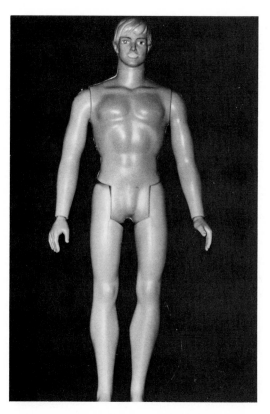

Ideal--7'' ''Baby, Baby'' One piece body and limbs of heavy vinyl. Beautiful toe and finger detail. Inset blue eyes with molded lashes. Open mouth/dry nurser. Put bottle in mouth and cheeks sink in like real feeding baby. Marks: 115/Ideal, in oval, 1974/B-6-B-52/Hong Kong. $5.00. (Courtesy Marie Ernst)

Ideal--12½'' ''Eric'', Tuesday Taylor's boyfriend. Rigid plastic body with rest vinyl, except hands. Bending elbows and knees. Jointed wrists, arms are ''ball jointed'' for sideward movement. Head looks much too small for body. Blonde molded hair and painted blue eyes to center. Marks: 1976 Ideal, in oval/Hollis N.Y. 11423/Hong Kong P. on lower back. $10.00.

 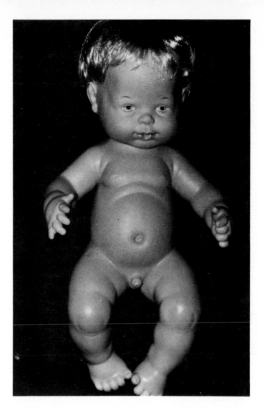

Ideal--16" "Tara" Plastic and vinyl with grow hair feature. Knob in center of back. Excellent finger detail. Marks: 1975/Ideal Toy Corp/H-250/Hong Kong, on head. 1970/Ideal Toy Corp/GH-15/M5169-01, on right hip. Made in Hong Kong, on left hip. $12.00. (Courtesy Phyllis Houston)

Ideal--15" "Joey Stivic", Archie Bunker's Grandson. All vinyl with one piece body and limbs. Painted blue eyes, open mouth/nurser. Marks: Ideal Toy Corp/J-14-H-253, on head. 1976/TYandem Prods. Inc./All Rights Reserved/Ideal, in oval, B-58, on back. Still available.

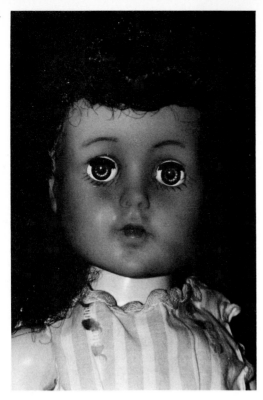

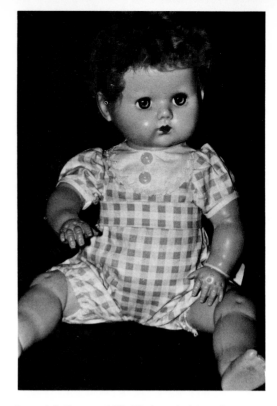

Imperial--17" "Linda" Heavy hard plastic with stuffed, early vinyl head. 1950. Sleep blue eyes/lashes. Closed mouth with serious expression. Glued on brown wig. Marks: Imperial, on head. $18.00.

Imperial Crown--15" "Baby Linda" All rubber body jointed at the shoulders and hips. Hard plastic head with sleep brown eyes/lashes. Open/closed mouth. Red caracul glued on wig. Marks: Imperial Crown Toy Co./Made in U.S.A. 1950. $16.00. (Courtesy Marie Ernst)

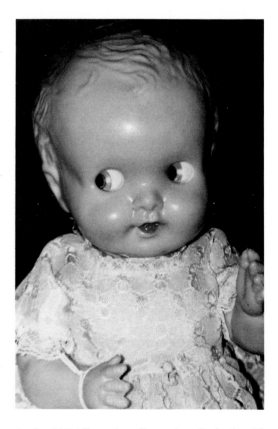

Imperial Crown--14" "Baby Perry" Hard plastic head with red caracul wig, sleep eyes/lashes and open mouth with felt tongue. One piece latex body and limbs. Original. Marks: Imperial Crown Toy Co./Made in U.S.A. 1951. $16.00. (Courtesy Anita Pacey)

Irwin--11" All good quality early soft plastic with one piece body and head. Molded hair. Blue painted eyes to side. Open Mouth/nurser. Bent baby legs. Marks: Irwin, in banner on back. $4.00. (Courtesy Marie Ernst)

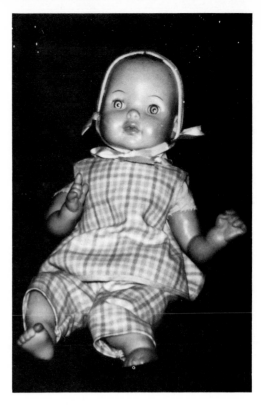

Irwin--6½" One piece plastic jointed at shoulders only. Eyes painted to side. Glued on hat over molded hair. Ad doll for Knotts Berry Farm. $2.00. (Courtesy Kathleen Flowers Council)

Jolly--19" "Mommy's Baby" Cloth body with vinyl limbs and head. Blue sleep eyes/lashes. Closed mouth. Rooted blonde hair (has been cut). Marks: 15/6/ Signature Doll/J T 1969, on head. Jolly Toys Inc./Skippy Doll Corp /Signature Doll Div./New York, N.Y. 1011, on tag. $4.00. (Photo courtesy Carolyn Powers)

Jolly Toys--11" Jolly Doll in it's original box. The doll is plastic with vinyl head, open/closed mouth and molded teeth. The blue eyes are painted. The head is from the Mattel Company and purchased by the Jolly Company. Marks: 1967/Mattel/-Japan, on head. 1975. Still available. (Courtesy Anita Pacey)

Junel--5½" "February's Birthday Girl" All composition. Jointed shoulders only. All original. Marks: None. Circa 1945. $7.00. (Courtesy Phyllis Houston)

Junel--7½'' ''Isabella'' All composition. No wig. Jointed hips and shoulders. Painted features. Flowers glued to forehead. Original. 1946. $10.00. (Courtesy Phyllis Houston)

Juro--24'' ''Pinky Lee'' Cloth with composition hands. Vinyl head and molded on hat. Inset brown eyes with open/closed mouth. Two pull rings in back, one operated arms and other legs. Marks: Juro/Celebrity/Product, on head. Pinky Lee/N.B.C. T.V., on jacket. Circa 1950's. $65.00. (Courtesy Virginia Jones)

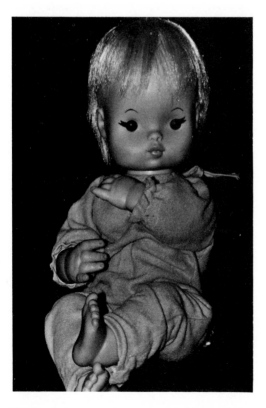

Kaybee--16'' ''Love-Lee'' Plastic with vinyl head and limbs. Painted black eyes. Bent baby legs. Good quality arms and legs. Original bunny suit. Marks: ⟨KB⟩   1966/deet, on head. Made by the

Kaybee--19'' ''Judy'' Plastic with vinyl head. Sleep blue eyes/lashes. Small up-turned nose. Slight cheek dimples. Rooted hair. Marks: ⟨KB⟩

Kaybee Doll & Toy Co. and designed by Deet. $6.00. (Courtesy Jayn Allen)

1966/deet, on head. Made by the Kaybee Doll & Toy Co. Designed by Deet. $5.00. (Courtesy Jayn Allen)

Kay Sam, Jolly--24" "Carol Channing" Plastic
and vinyl. Sleep blue eyes with blue eyeshadow.
Marks: 1961/KAYSAM, on doll. ANOTHER
JOLLY TOY, on tag. $165.00. (Courtesy Marie
Ernst)

15" "GiGi" (Juliet Prowse) Plastic and vinyl with
rooted blonde short hair, blue sleep eyes with
wash eyeshadow. Red taffeta dress, white
bloomers and black garter with red rose. Marks:
Kaysam 1961. $65.00.

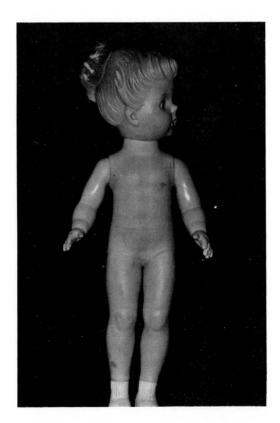

Kay Sam--13" "Patty Girl" All vinyl with one
piece body and legs. Inset eyes. Molded bun on
back of head and panties, shoes and socks.
Marks: K, circle C, on lower back. KAYSAM
CORP/40, on foot. 1955. $3.00. (Courtesy Marie
Ernst)

Kay Sam--17" "Barbara" Plastic body and legs.
Vinyl head and arms. Almost white rooted hair.
Sleep blue eyes. Open/closed mouth. Dimples.
Hands down with right hand all fingers separate.
Left hand with 2nd & 3rd fingers molded
together. 1963. Marks: 4269/K27, on head.
6514/KAYSAM, on lower back. $8.00. (Courtesy
Phyllis Houston.

Kenner--6" "Sippin' Sam" All vinyl with jointed shoulders & neck. Round hole in mouth for straw. Hands cupped to fit edge of cup. Marks: KENNER PRODUCTS/DIV. G.M.F.G.I. CINN./HONG KONG. 1972. $2.00.

Kenner--6" "Sippin' Bam Bam" All vinyl. Jointed neck & shoulders. Round hole at mouth for straw. Hands cupped to fit over rim of cup. Marks: Can't make out top line/KENNER PRODUCTS/DIV. G.M.F.G.I. CINN./HONG KONG. 1972. $3.00.

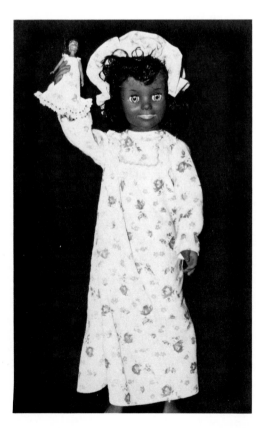

Kenner--17" "Sleep Over Dolly" Plastic with vinyl arms and head. Brown sleep eyes/lashes. Open/closed teeth are painted white. Came with tiny Skye doll. The white version of this doll comes with a tiny Dusty doll. Marks: G.M.F.G.I./1976, on back of head. The tiny doll is 3¾" and all one piece vinyl with adult figure. Marks: None. $12.00.

Kenner--Miniture Skye doll that comes with the Sleep Over Dolly, with case containing overnight accessories for the large doll. (Courtesy Phyllis Houston)

Little bisque dolls (shown) marked with K & H
were made by the Santa Clara Tile Company
(California) during World War II and the factory
was condemned in 1968 but not torn down until
1973. The dolls were found to be stored in the
building to be demolished and sold to collectors.
The basic 7'' doll has joints at the shoulders only
and was called "Peg of My Heart". They came in
boxes with both pink and blue dots. There is a
baby that is 4'' tall and jointed at the hips and the
shoulders. These babies came undressed and also
in a little fitted pink flannel bunting. A few of
these babies were 5'' in size.

The Kerr & Hinz dolls shown in the following
two photos are courtesy of Kathryn Fain. 5''
$18.00. 7'' $23.00.

Knickerbocher--10½" "Carrie" with freckles and brown painted eyes. Marks: K.T.D./A.G.C./ 1974. Still available. (Courtesy Marie Ernst)

Knickerbocher--10½" Left: Amy with light freckles and blue painted eyes. Right is Holly Hobbie with round face, light freckles and painted brown eyes. Marks: K.T.D./A.G.C./ 1974. Still available. (Courtesy Marie Ernst)

Knickerbocher--7" "Sunbonnet Dolls" This one is Mandy. Marks: K.T.C./Made in Taiwan/1975, on head. Still available.

Knickerbocher--7" "Sunbonnet Dolls" All vinyl with painted eyes. Original. Left to right: May & Molly. Followed by Mandy. Marks: K.T.C./Made in Taiwan/1975. Still available. (Courtesy Connie Chase)

Knickerbocher--6½" "Amy" All vinyl. Fully jointed. Removable clothes. Tiny painted eyes. 2" vinyl baby that is all one piece. Comes with bottle & rattle, baby & buggy. Marks: KTC/AGC/ MADE IN TAIWAN/1975, on head. HOLLY HOBBIE/AGC 1975/MADE IN TAIWAN/ KTC, on back. Baby is marked: AG/KTC, on back. Still available.

Knickerbocher--6½" "Holly Hobbie" All vinyl. Fully jointed. Removable clothes. Comes with wagon, water can & two potted plants. Marks: KTC/AGC/MADE IN TAIWAN/KTC, on back. Still available.

Knickerbocher--6½" "Carrie" All vinyl. Fully jointed. Removable clothes. Comes with all vinyl cat, plastic table, stool, cup, bowl and 2 utensils. Marks: KTC/AGC/ 1975/MADE IN TAIWAN/KTC, on back. Still available.

Knickerbocher--11" "Missy" All vinyl with very little feature detail. Painted eyes. Original. Marks: K.T.C. 1975/Made in Taiwan, on head and back. Still available.

Knickerbocher--10½'' by 9¾'' ''Holly Hobbie Tote 'N Doll Bag'' Has a 7'' Holly Hobbie doll in pocket. Still available. (Courtesy 1975 Knickerbocher catalog)

Knickerbocher--16'' ''Tom Sawyer'' & ''Becky Thatcher'' (14½'') $6.00 each. (Courtesy Knickerbocher 1975 catalog)

Knickerbocher--11'' ''Little Wigwams'' $7.00 each. (Courtesy Knickerbocher 1975 catalog)

Knickerbocher-- 10'' ''Love Is'' dolls. Still available in some areas. (Courtesy Knickerbocher 1975 catalog)

Knickerbocher--11" "Hairy Scareys" Left to right: Frankie Baby, Wacky Wolf, Simple Simian & Count Drooly. $6.00 each. (Courtesy Knickerbocher 1975 catalog)

Knickerbocher--6" "Bride and Groom Dolls" are rattles for a baby. MIB. Hard shiny plastic with painted on shoes and socks. Fully jointed. Marks: Knickerbocher/Plastic Co./Glendale, Calif./Des. Pat./Pending, on back. $6.00. (Courtesy Phyllis Houston)

Knickerbocher-- 15" rag and vinyl. (vinyl hands). Marks: Knickerbocher/19(C)65/Japan. $5.00. (Courtesy Phyllis Houston)

Knickerbocher Plastic Co.--6'' All plastic. Jointed shoulders only. Painted black eyes. Molded hair. Place for bow. Oil cloth clothes someone made. Marks: KNICKERBOCHER/PLASTIC CO./GLENDALE CALIF./DES. PAT/PENDING. The Knickerbocher Plastic Co. was purchased by Eldon Industries in November, 1960. $3.00.

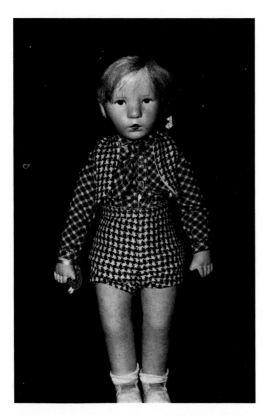

Kruse, Kathe--14'' Late Kruse boy ''Jorgeh'' with side part hair. 1966. All cloth with painted features. Flat stitched fingers. Tag on wrist. $45.00. (Courtesy Jay Minter)

Lander--9½'' Left: ''Betty Bubbles'' & right: ''Angelique'' Both have one piece bottle bodies & limbs. Heads are vinyl with rooted hair and painted eyes. Marks: Japan, on head. Sticker on bottom says made by Lander. 1967. $2.00 each.

Lee, H.D.--13'' ''Black Magic'' (Buddy Lee doll) All composition with one piece body and head. Painted on shoes. In original Engineer outfit with ''Black Magic'' on cap. Made for ''Gundy Duncers'' (line workers) on spur line of Union Pacific in 1946. $125.00. $165.00 (Photo courtesy Mrs. Ernestine Howard)

Majber--18'' ''Lindy'' Plastic with vinyl head. Has deep skin coloring, very thick dark rooted hair & light blue sleep eyes. Open/closed mouth. Original nylon bodysuit with red ''suede'' Balero & skirt. Marks: MAJBER, on head. 1966. $10.00. (Courtesy Phyllis Houston)

Mfg. Unknown--15'' ''Popeye'' (King Features) Composition and wood. Jointed shoulders, neck and hips. Marks: None. $22.00. (Courtesy Phyllis Houston)

Mfg. Unknown--15'' ''Shirley Temple'' All very heavy, solid rubber (Guta purcha). Sleep green eyes/lashes. Dimples and open mouth with four teeth. The paint crazes like on some of the Effanbee's early Anne Shirleys arms. Marks: 7, front of neck; 4, upper leg; 7, on upper other leg. Has holes in feet. $45.00. (Courtesy Virginia Jones)

157

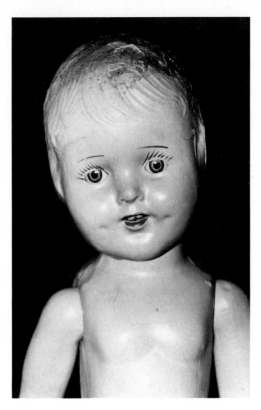

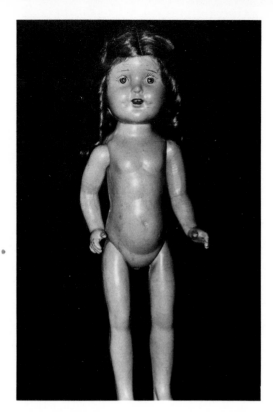

Mfg. Unknown--15" All composition Shirley Temple look-a-like. Molded Patsy style hair. Sleep tin blue eyes, dimples and open mouth with two upper teeth. $45.00. (Courtesy Kathy Walker)

Shows the body construction of the 15" Shirley Temple look-a-like doll with original wig. (Courtesy Kathy Walter)

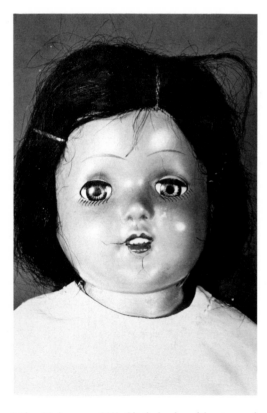

Mfg. Unknown--24" "Baby Pam" Painted hard plastic head. Sleep blue eyes/lashes. Open mouth with two upper teeth. Cloth body with latex arms & legs. Glued on mohair wig. Original. Marks: AXAX, on head. 1953. $18.00. (Courtesy Betty Snider)

Mfg. Unknown--22" Cloth body with composition shoulder plate and swivel head. Sleep brown eyes/lashes. Open mouth/four upper teeth. Human hair wig. Full composition legs and arms. Marks: None. $28.00. (Courtesy Betty Kirtley)

Mfg. Unknown--11'' All hard plastic. Molded, painted hair, blue eyes and shoes/socks. Open mouth. Fully jointed with palms down. See following photos for back of head and contents. Action unknown. $16.00. (Courtesy Phyllis Houston)

Mfg. Unknown--This is view of the back of the head of the 11' hard plastic girl.

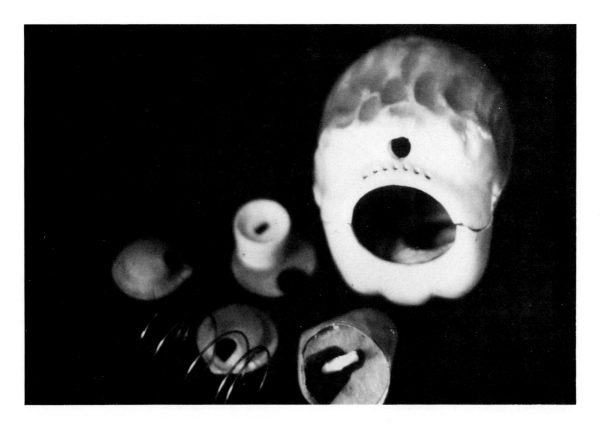

Mfg. Unknown--This is the contents of the head of the 11'' hard plastic girl. Action unknown.

Ideal--11½'' ''Helen Walker'' All hard plastic walker. Sleep blue eyes/molded lashes. Glued on saran wig. Marks: None. 1963. $9.00. (Courtesy Anita Pacey)

17'' ''Unknown'' This is the Margaret O'Brien dressed in really fine quality clothes that are silver and gold. The cape is green with stand up collar and has a silver lining. The hair is black and she has portrait painted features and nails. $95.00. (Courtesy Jeannie Gregg)

Mfg. Unknown--3¼'' Plastic ''Bathing Beauty'' Standing with purple suit. Gold painted sandels. Marks: None. $6.00. (Courtesy Barbara Monzelluzzi)

Mfg. Unknown--1¾'' tall and 2½'' long sitting ''Bathing Beauty'' Red suit. Marks: None. $6.00. (Courtesy Barabara Monzelluzzi)

Mfg. Unknown--6" "Nancy" All rubber. Painted clothes & features. $5.00. (Courtesy Barbara Monteguzzi)

Mfg. Unknown--15" "Old Smuggler Scotch Whisky" advertising doll. Vinyl with painted features and shoes. Removable clothes. $22.00. (Courtesy Yvonne Baird)

Mfg. Unknown--11½" "Dondi" One piece body and limbs. All vinyl with neck jointed only. Dressed in red/white and blue. Marks: 1960/Chicago Trib. N.Y. News Synd. 1955. $35.00. (Courtesy Virginia Jones)

Mfg. Unknown--10½" "Indian" with rooted blonde hair, lovely painted eyes. All vinyl and fully jointed. Marks: None. $4.00. (Courtesy Phyllis Houston)

M & S--10½'' ''Pug'' All vinyl with red ''butch'' molded hair and painted black eyes to the side. Marks: M & S Doll, on head. 1961. $6.00. (Courtesy Jayn Allen)

Marlon--8'' ''Sussy'' All vinyl jointed at shoulders, hips and neck. Sleep eyes. Open mouth/nurser. Original bunny suit. 1968. $4.00. (Courtesy Louise Ceglia)

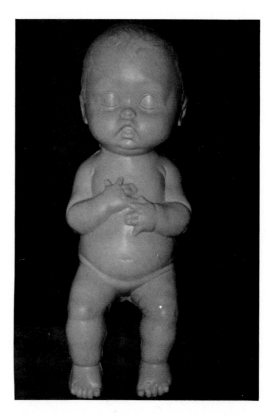

Marlon--Shows the back of the original bunny suit on the Marlon baby. (Courtesy Louise Ceglia)

Marx--16'' ''Baby'' that is all one piece with decal eyes. Marks: Louis Marx & Co. Inc./MCMLX-V/Patent Pending. $4.00. (Courtesy Florence Black Musich)

Mattel--Tiny Chatty Baby outfit #283. 1962. $3.00.

Mattel--15" "Chester O'Chimp" All plush stuffed. Wired fingers. Vinyl head and ears. Eyes twirl. Mouth will open wide. Pull string talker. Marks:MATTEL/CHESTER O'CHIMP/ 1964 MATTEL INC. HAWTHORNE, CALIF., on tag. $6.00. $5.00. (Courtesy of 5 yr. old Steve Malicoat)

Mattel--11" "T-Bone" Cloth. Pull string talker. Vinyl head with painted features. Marks: None on doll. T-BONE TM 1964 MATTEL INC., on tag. $5.00.

Mattel--2" "Santa" All one piece vinyl. Painted features. Marks: M.I., on head. $3.00.

Mattel--2" Storybook Kiddles, "Rapunzel and the Prince" Come with storybook and jewelery. 1966. $10.00.

Mattel--2" Storybook Kiddles, "Sweethearts Robin and Maid Marion" Comes with storybook and jewelery. 1966. $10.00.

Mattel--2" Kiddle Sweethearts, "Romeo and Juliet" Comes with storybook and jewelery. 1966. $10.00.

Mattel--2" Storybook Kiddles, "King and Queen of Hearts" Comes with storybook and jewelery. 1966. $10.00.

Mattel--"Mini-Kiddles Popup Soda Parlor" 1967. $3.00.

Mattel--18" "Gentle Ben" Plush pull string talker. Plastic eyes, nose with felt tongue. Marks: MATTEL/GENTLE BEN/1967 IVAN TORS/FILMS INC., on tag. $6.00.

Mattel--3½" "Rolly Twiddle" On the market in 1967-68. All vinyl Kiddle. Came with wagon, pail & shovel. Dark brown hair and brown painted eyes. Marks: MATTEL, INC., on head. $7.00. (Courtesy Joan Asherbraner)

Mattel--2" "Lois Locket" #3723. On market 1968. Green dress & locket. Marks: Mattel Inc., on head. $12.00. (Courtesy Joan Asherbraner)

Mattel--12" "Push-Me-Pull Yu" All plush with felt features. Talker, pull string operated. Marks: 1967/MATTEL/JAPAN, on tag. $4.00.

Mattel--11" "Sexed Girl" Soft plastic body with rest vinyl. Blue sleep eyes/lashes. Upper lip protrudes. Excellent hand and feet detail. Marks: RATTI/MADE IN ITALY, on head. S (backward) P (backward) A/ MATTEL/MADE IN ITALY, on back. Ratti factory in Italy is one that Mattel, inc. purchased. $18.00. (Courtesy Phyllis Houston)

Mattel--8" "Baby Fun" All vinyl with open mouth, painted eyes and rooted hair. By pressing body, she blows up ballons and party favors. Original dress. Marks: 1968 Mattel Inc./Hong Kong, on head. Patent Pending/1968 Mattel Inc. /Hong Kong, on lower back. 1968 Mattel, on dress tag. $4.00.

Mattel--24" "Black Dancerina" Plastic body and legs. Vinyl arms and head. Brown painted eyes. Knob on top of head. Marks: 1968/Mattel, on head and body. $16.00. (Courtesy Betty Kirtley)

Mattel--3½" "Tangie" rag doll that goes with the Angie N' Tangie set of 1969. Cloth with vinyl head. Stitched on yarn hair. Large painted blue eyes, rose spots on cheeks & watermelon, smile mouth. Original. Marks: None. $4.00. $3.00.

Mattel--17" "Tinker Bell" Printed all over foam. Pull string talker. Cloth/wire wings. Marks: WALT DISNEY PRODUCTIONS. MADE BY MATTEL INC. MADE IN MEXICO 1968, on tag. $4.00.

Mattel-19" "Bugs Bunny" Plush with vinyl face & hands/carrot. Pull string talker. Marks: MATTEL/BUGS BUNNY WARNER BROS. PICTURES, INC. 1969. $6.00.

Mattel--15" "Platter Pal" Cloth. Pull string talker. Marks: MATTEL/A PLATTER PAL/1969 MATTEL INC, on tag. $4.00.

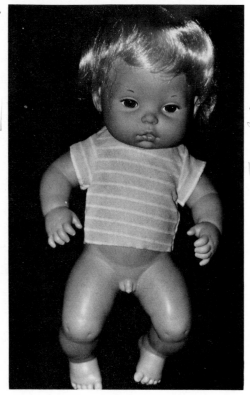

Mattel--13" "Baby Brother Tenderlove" One piece Dublon body. Anatomically correct (sexed). Vinyl head with decal brown eyes. Open mouth/nurser. Marks: 1972 Mattel Inc., on head. 1975 Mattel Inc. U.S.A., on back. Still available.

Mattel--15" "Baby That Away" Plastic with vinyl head. Jointed knees. Painted brown eyes. Closed mouth. Battery operated. Walks, crawls & fusses. Marks: MATTEL INC. 1974/U.S.A./ U.S. Patents Pending, on back. Mattel Inc. 1974 U.S.A., on head. Still available. (Courtesy Phyllis Houston)

Mattel--10" "Mama Beans" & 4" "Twins". Mama is cloth with vinyl head. Hair is rooted and pulled to back in a bun. Bonnet is stitched on. Marks: 1974 Mattel Inc., on head. Mattel Mama Beans & Baby Beans 1975, on tag. Twins have full vinyl head with no hair except five painted curls on front. Cloth stuffed body. Marks: 1975 Mattel Inc., on head and same tag as Mama. Still available.

Mattel--5" "Sweetie" and 4" "Lil Kid" Sweeties box says: I make the yummiest cookies in the world and Lil Kid says: Me'n Good Dog wanta play, too. Marks: Same as Slugger. Still available.

Mattel--4½'' "I.Q." and 6'' "Solo" I.Q. has brown eyes and an oriental cast face with glasses atop head. Solo is Colored. I.Q.'s box says: I always get straight A's in school and Solo's box says: I'm practicing to be a great musician. Marks: Both same as on Slugger. Still available.

Mattel--5½'' "Darlin'" and 6'' "Spunky" Spunky has a dimple in the right cheek and freckles. Darlin's box says: I'm soooo pretty! Don't you agree and Spunky's box says: Nobody bosses me 'cuz I'm tuff. Marks: Both same as on Slugger. Still available.

Mattel--5½'' "Slugger" Vinyl head with rooted red hair. Painted green eyes, freckles and stuffed body and limbs. Marks: 1975 MATTEL INC./TAIWAN. MATTEL INC. 1975/HAW THORNE, CALIF/90250/MADE IN TAIWAN, on tag. One box says: I can hit more "homers" than anybody! Still available.

Mattel--11½'' "Medaille D' or Barbie" Same doll as the American Barbie but the medal has an oak leaf and has different shape. Marks: 1966/Mattel Inc./US & Foreign/Patented/Other Pats./Pending/Made in Taiwan. Young Olympians of Canada, in English and in French, on box. 1976. $12.00. (Courtesy Marie Ernst)

Mattel--This is the Mattel 1976-77 Black Happy Family Grandparents. Still available.

Mattel--11½" "Sweet 16" Vinyl head, rest is rigid plastic with non-bendable legs. Large painted brown eyes. Marks: 1/MATTEL INC./1958/KOREA. Stock No. 9537. Mattel Inc. 1975, Hawthorne, Calif. 90250, on box. Made and printed in Korea. (Courtesy Phyllis Houston)

Mattel--6" "Buffy" and 3½" "Mrs. Beasley" Uses the Tutti body. Vinyl head with blue eyes and freckles. Original. Tag on Mrs. Beasley: Mrs. Beasley/1967 Family Affair Co./1967 Mattel/Inc. Japan. Tiny glasses are missing. $14.00. (Courtesy Laura Gann)

Mattel--20" "Black Chatty Cathy" Mattel did not make a great quanity of these Black Chatty Cathys and therefore they are considered rare. $95.00. (Courtesy Irene Gann)

Mattel--18" "Barbie" Plastic with vinyl head. Legs and arms are molded in position. Jointed waist. Comes with own stand, long skirt and pants (long). 1977. Marks: Taiwan/1976 Mattel, on head. Matter Inc. 1976 U.S.A., on body.

Mattel--6" "Hayseed" and 5" "Long Dog, Chum" Part of the Honey Hill Bunch. Dog is felt and plush with vinyl head and has velour strips to hold Hayseed on his back. Marks: 1976 Mattel Inc. Taiwan, on head. He is all cloth with vinyl head and has freckles. Marks: 1975 Mattel Inc. Japan, on head.

MEGO

The following listing was made up and the work of Joe Bourgious and in going over the list, the collector can just how many and varied are the dolls from this company.

MODEL #	SIZE	NAME & PARTICULARS	MOLD MARK & LOCATION	YEAR

ACTION JACKSON SERIES

√ 1100	8''	ACTION JACKSON (WHITE) Black molded hair, black eyes, NO beard.	**On Shoulder Blades** © Mego Corp. Reg. U.S. Pat. Off. Pat. Pending Hong Kong MCMLXXI	1972
1132	8''	ACTION JACKSON (WHITE) Black molded hair, black eyes, black beard.	**On Shoulder Blades** © Mego Corp. Reg. U.S. Pat. Off. Pat. Pending Hong Kong MCMLXXI	1972
1133	8''	ACTION JACKSON (BLACK) Black molded hair, black eyes, NO beard.	**On Shoulder Blades** © Mego Corp. Reg. U.S. Pat. Off. Pat. Pending Hong Kong MCMLXXI	1972

DINAH-MITE SERIES

1400	8''	DINAH-MITE (WHITE) Rooted blonde hair, blue eyes.	**On Shoulder Blades** © Mego Corp. MCMLXXII Pat. Pending Made In Hong Kong	1973
1400	8''	DINAH-MITE (BLACK) Rooted black hair, black eyes.	**On Shoulder Blades** © Mego Corp. MCMLXXII Pat. Pending Made In Hong Kong	1973

WORLD GREATEST SUPER HEROES SERIES

1300	8''	SUPERMAN	**On Shoulder Blades** © Mego Corp. Reg. U.S. Pat. Off. Pat. Pending Hong Kong MCMLXXI	1973
1301	8''	BATMAN	**On Shoulder Blades** © Mego Corp. Reg. U.S. Pat. Off. Pat. Pending Hong Kong MCMLXXI	1973
1302	8''	ROBIN	**On Shoulder Blades** © Mego Corp. Reg. U.S. Pat. Off. Pat. Pending Hong Kong MCMLXXI	1973
1303	8''	AQUAMAN	**On Shoulder Blades** © Mego Corp. Reg. U.S. Pat. Off. Pat. Pending Hong Kong MCMLXXI	1973

1304	8"	CAPTAIN AMERICA	**On Shoulder Blades** © Mego Corp. Reg. U.S. Pat. Off. Pat. Pending Hong Kong MCMLXXI	1973
1305	8"	TARZAN	**On Shoulder Blades** © Mego Corp. Reg. U.S. Pat. Off. Pat. Pending Hong Kong MCMLXXI	1973
1306	8"	SPIDER MAN	**On Shoulder Blades** © Mego Corp. Reg. U.S. Pat. Off. Pat. Pending Hong Kong MCMLXXI	1973
1307	8"	SHAZAM	**On Shoulder Blades** © Mego Corp. Reg. U.S. Pat. Off. Pat. Pending Hong Kong MCMLXXI	1973

WORLD GREATEST SUPER HEROES "ARCH ENEMY" SERIES

1350	8"	PENGUIN	**On Shoulder Blades** Hong Kong Mego Corp. © 1973	1974
1351	8"	JOKER	**On Shoulder Blades** © Mego Corp. Reg. U.S. Pat. Off. Pat. Pending Hong Kong MCMLXXI	1974
1352	8"	RIDDLER	**On Shoulder Blades** © Mego Corp. Reg. U.S. Pat. Off. Pat. Pending Hong Kong MCMLXXI	1974
1353	8"	MR. MXYZPTLK	**On Shoulder Blades** Hong Kong Mego Corp. © 1973	1974

WORLD GREATEST SUPER GALS SERIES

| 1341 | 8" | WONDER WOMEN | **On Shoulder Blades**
© Mego Corp.
MCMLXXII
Pat. Pending
Made In
Hong Kong | 1974 |
| 1342 | 8" | SUPER GIRL | **On Shoulder Blades**
© Mego Corp.
MCMLXXII
Pat. Pending
Made In
Hong Kong | 1974 |

| 1343 | 8" | BAT GIRL | **On Shoulder Blades** © Mego Corp. MCMLXXII Pat. Pending Made In Hong Kong | 1974 |
| 1344 | 8" | CAT WOMEN | **On Shoulder Blades** © Mego Corp. MCMLXXII Pat. Pending Made In Hong Kong | 1974 |

WORLD GREATEST SUPER HEROES! THE MAD MONSTER SERIES

1900	**8"**	**FRANKENSTEIN**	**On Shoulder Blades** © Mego Corp. Reg. U.S. Pat. Off. Pat. Pending Hong Kong MCMLXXI	1974
1901	8"	DRACULA	**On Shoulder Blades** © Mego Corp. Reg. U.S. Pat. Off. Pat. Pending Hong Kong MCMLXXI	1974
1902	8"	WOLFMAN	**On Shoulder Blades** © Mego Corp. Reg. U.S. Pat. Off. Pat. Pending Hong Kong MCMLXXI	1974
1903	8"	MUMMY	**On Shoulder Blades** © Mego Corp. Reg. U.S. Pat. Off. Pat. Pending Hong Kong MCMLXXI	1974

WORLD GREATEST SUPER HEROES! "WILD WEST" SERIES

1360	8"	WYATT EARP	**On Shoulder Blades** © Mego Corp. Reg. U.S. Pat. Off. Pat. Pending Hong Kong MCMLXXI	1974
1361	8"	COCHISE	**On Shoulder Blades** © Mego Corp. Reg. U.S. Pat. Off. Pat. Pending Hong Kong MCMLXXI	1974
1362	8"	DAVEY CROCKET	**On Shoulder Blades** © Mego Corp. Reg. U.S. Pat. Off. Pat. Pending Hong Kong MCMLXXI	1974
1363	8"	BUFFALO BILL CODY	**On Shoulder Blades** © Mego Corp. Reg. U.S. Pat. Off. Pat. Pending Hong Kong MCMLXXI	1974

| 1364 | 8" | WILD BILL HICKOK | **On Shoulder Blades** © Mego Corp. Reg. U.S. Pat. Off. Pat. Pending Hong Kong MCMLXXI | 1974 |
| 1365 | 8" | SITTING BULL | **On Shoulder Blades** © Mego Corp. Reg. U.S. Pat. Off. Pat. Pending Hong Kong MCMLXXI | 1974 |

MOVIE PLANET OF THE APES SERIES

1961	8"	CORNELIUS
1962	8"	DR. ZAIUS
1963	8"	ZIRA
1964	8"	SOLDIER APE
1965	8"	ASTRNAULT

MODEL ©	SIZE	NAME & PARTICULARS	MOLD MARK & LOCATION	YEAR

STAR TREK SERIES

51200/1	8"	CAPT. KIRK
51200/2	8"	MR. SPOCK
51200/3	8"	DR. McCOY (BONES)
51200/4	8"	LT. UHURA
51200/5	8"	MR. SCOTT (SCOTTIE)
51200/7	8"	KLINGTON

WIZARD OF OZ SERIES

51500/1	8"	DOROTHY & TOTO
51500/2	8"	TIN WOODSMAN
51500/3	8"	COWARDLY LION
51500/4	8"	SCARECROW
51500/5	8"	GLINDA "THE GOOD WITCH"
51500/6	8"	WICKED WITCH
	8"	WIZARD

CAMELOT SERIES

51000/1	8"	KING ARTHUR
51000/3	8"	SIR GALAHAD
51000/4	8"	SIR LANCELOT
51000/5	8"	BLACK KNIGHT
51000/6	8"	IVAN HOE

ROBIN HOOD SERIES

51100/1	8"	ROBIN HOOD
51100/2	8"	LITTLE JOHN
51100/3	8"	FRIAR TUCK
51100/4	8"	WILL SCARLET

WORLD'S GREATEST SUPER HEROES

51300/1	8"	GREEN ARROW
51300/2	8"	GREEN GOBLIN
51300/3	8"	THE LIZARD (Spider Man's Arch Enemy)
51300/4	8"	THE FALCON
51300/5	8"	THE INVINCIBLE IRON MAN
51300/6	8"	THE INCREDIBLE HULK
51304	8"	CAPTAIN AMERICA
51306	8"	SPIDER MAN

THE WALTON SERIES (Two Dolls Per Package)

56000/1	8''	JOHN BOY &		1975
56000/1	8''	ELLEN		1975
56000/2	8''	MOM	**On Head** ©1974 Lorimar Inc. **On Back** © Mego Corp. MCMLXXII Pat. Pending Made In Hong Kong	1975
56000/2	8''	POP	**On Head** ©1974 Lorimar Inc. **On Back** © Mego Corp. MCMLXXII Pat. Pending Made In Hong Kong	1975
56000/3	8''	GRANDMA	**On Head** ©1974 Lorimar Prod. Inc. **On Back** © Mego Corp. 1974 Reg. U.S. Pat. Off. Pat. Pending Hong Kong	1975
56000/3	8''	GRANDPA	**On Head** ©1974 Lorimar Prod. Inc. **On Back** © Mego Corp. 1974 Reg. U.S. Pat. Off. Pat. Pending Hong Kong	1974

PIRATE SERIES

54000/2	8''	CAPTAIN PATCH
54000/3	8''	JEAN LAFITTE
54000/4	8''	LONG JOHN SILVER
54000/5	8''	BLACKBEARD

WORLD'S GREATEST SUPER HEROES

51313/1	8''	THE MIGHTY THOR
51313/2	8''	CONAN
51313/3	8''	THE THING
51313/4	8''	THE HUMAN TORCH
51313/5	8''	MISTER FANTASTIC
51313/6	8''	THE INVISIBLE GIRL

STAR TREK ALIENS SERIES

51203/1	8''	NEPRUNAIN
51203/2	8''	THE KEEPER
51203/3	8''	THE GORN
51203/4	8''	THE CHERON

ONE MILLION B.C. SERIES

✓ 62600/1	8"	TRAG	
✓ 62600/2	8"	MADA	
✓ 62600/3	8"	GROK	
62600/4	8"	ZON	
✓ 62600/5	8"	ORM	

on head
© *1975 MEGO CORP*
on back
© *MEGO CORP 1974*
PAT PEND
HONG KONG

MODEL #	**SIZE**	**NAME & PARTICULARS**	**MOLD MARK & LOCATION**	**YEAR**

OUR GANG SERIES

61600/1	5"	ALFALFA
61600/2	5"	SPANKY
61600/3	5"	BUCKWHEAT
61600/4	5"	DORLA
61600/5	5"	MICKEY
61600/6	5"	PORKY

T.V. PLANET OF THE APE SERIES

50900/6	8"	GALEN
50900/7	8"	GENERAL URSUS
50900/8	8"	GENERAL URKO
50900/9	8"	PETER BURKE
50900/0	8"	ALAN VERDON

WORLD'S GREATEST SUPER HEROES FIST FIGHTING SERIES

51600/1	8"	FIST FIGHTING BATMAN
51600/2	8"	FIST FIGHTING ROBIN
51600/5	8"	FIST FIGHTING RIDDLER
51600/6	8"	FIST FIGHTING JOKER

Mego--"The Waltons" Marks: 1974 Lorimor/Prod. Inc. Left to right: Grandma, Grandpa, Ma, Pa, Mary Ellen, Jon Boy. $6.00 each. (Courtesy Connie Chase)

Mego--8" "Mr. Fantastic" Plastic with vinyl head. Full action figure. Molded grey-black hair. Marks: 1975 Marvel/C.G., on head. Mego Corp./Reg. U.S. Pat. Off./Pat. Pending/Hong Kong, on back. $4.00.

Mego--8" "The Invisable Girl" Plastic with vinyl head. Full jointed action figure. Blonde rooted hair. Open/closed mouth with painted teeth. Blue painted eyes. Marks: 1974 Marvel/C.G., on head. Mego Corp/MCMLXXII,/Pat. Pending/Made In/Hong Kong, on back. $4.00.

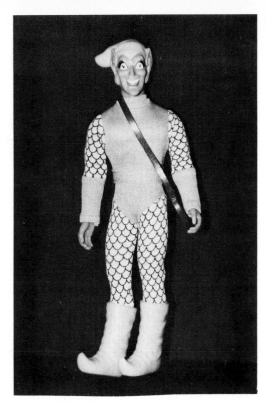

Mego--11½" "Dr. Kromedome, The Bionic Villian" Full action figure except arms. Left arm is all silver. Bald with silver helmet. Painted lines on face. Marks: MEGO CORP./1975, on head. MADE IN HONG KONG, on back. $10.00.

Mego--8" "Green Goblin" Fully jointed action figure. He is Spider-man's Arch Enemy. All original. $4.00. (Courtesy Marie Ernst)

Mego--8" "Iron Man" Fully jointed action figure. Removable clothes. $4.00. (Courtesy Marie Ernst)

Mego--8" "Wolfman" Fully jointed action figure. Eyes and hands glow in the dark. Marks: MEGO CORP, on head. $4.00. (Courtesy Marie Ernst)

Mego--8" "The Falcon" Fully jointed action figure. Black man. Marks: MEGO CORP., on head. $4.00. (Courtesy Marie Ernst)

Mego--7" "Hulk" Jointed elbows & knees. Marks: MEGO CORP., on head. $4.00. (Courtesy Marie Ernst)

Mego--8" "Conan" (of Fantastic 4). Plastic with vinyl head. Full jointed action figure. Open/closed mouth with painted teeth. Rooted hair. Marks: 1975/Marvel C.G., on head. MEGO CORP./ Reg. U.S. Pat. Off./Pat. Pending/Hong Kong, on back. Conan is a character created by Robert E. Howard. $4.00.

Mego--8" "Human Torch" Plastic with vinyl head, full action figure. Skin tones are all red. Marks: Marvel, on head. Mego Corp./ Reg. U.S. Pat. Off./Pat. Pending/Hong Kong, on back. $4.00.

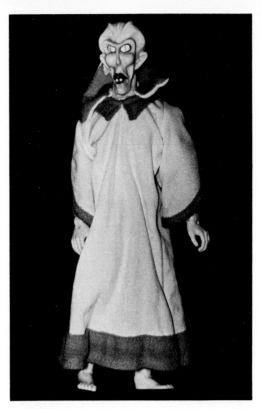

Mego--8" "The Gorn", a Star Trek Alien. Full action figure. Marks: 1974 Paramount Pict./Corp./Mego Corp. 1974, on head. Reg. U.S. Pat. Off./Pat. Pending/Hong Kong, on back. $4.00.

Mego--8" "The Keeper", a Star Trek Alien. Full action figure. Marks: Paramount Prod./Corp./Mego Corp 1974, on head. Reg. U.S. Pat. Off./Pat. Pending/Hong Kong, on back. $4.00.

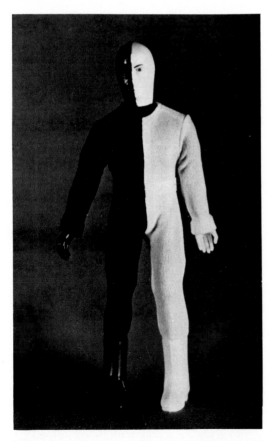

Mego--8" "Cheron", a Star Trek Alien. Plastic full action figure with vinyl head painted half black and white to match outfit. Marks: 1974 Paramount Prod./Corp./Mego Corp./1974, on head. Reg. U.S. Pat. Off./Pat. Pending/Hong Kong, on back. $4.00.

Mego--8" "The Thing" Orange full action figure that has extra joints at the wrists and waist but the ankles are not jointed. Marks: 1975 Marvel C.G., on head. Mego Corp 1974/Reg. U.S. Pat. Off./Pat. Pending/Hong Kong, on back. $4.00. (Courtesy Marie Ernst)

Mego--15" "Wizard of Oz Dolls" that were made in a very limited number by Mego and never put on the general market. They have cloth bodies with vinyl heads. Marks: Mego. $16.00 each.

Mego--12½" "Farrah-Fawcett Majors" Same body as used for Cher doll. Bending Knees. Marks: Mego Corp. 1975/Made in Hong Kong. The head is vinyl with vivid green decal eyes and open/closed mouth. Long inset lashes. Comes in two different hair colors. Marked: Farrah, on head. $8.00.

Mego--9½" "Muhammad Ali" Heavy vinyl doll with plastic attached belt that is operated by trigger attached to back of belt. Bendable knees. Jointed ankles, waist and wrists. Marks: Mego Corp./New York, N.Y./Patent Pending/Made in Hong Kong/, on lower torso. H.M. ENT./1975, on head. Everlast, on belt. $8.00.

MOLLYE

Mollye Goldman, whose real first name is Marysia, was born near Odessa, Russia near the turn of this century. When she was a very small girl, her parents fled with her to the United States. She was hand sewing everything she saw from age six and grew up to be internationally known as the most prolific and imaginative designer of doll clothes and dolls.

Mollye married Myer Goldman in 1919, and began commercially, making dolls shortly after that. It was in 1933, that Mollye saw Shirley Temple for the first time and thought she was such a beautiful child that she knew she could make a doll dressed just like her.

Mollye showed a completed doll (not a Shirley doll) at the Toy Fair in 1933, where the president of Ideal Doll Co. saw it. "Maybe I'm crazy but I think she is beautiful, too!," he stated, and the contract was made. Mollye traveled around the country on a good-will tour and pushed promotions. Within five months, the Shirley Temple doll was a two and half million dollar baby. By 1934, Gimbels (New York) employed 8 demonstrators just to sell the doll's clothes. The actual doll was designed by Bernard Lipford.

Mollye's business actually began as a home sewing one, on Regent Street in West Philadelphia and says, "We were the only Jewish couple in an Irish neighborhood and they just treat you great. All the women in the neighborhood sewed for me. Some put their children through college on those wages. When the business expanded we operated from a factory at 68th and Woodland. At one time we had 500 people working."

Mollye not only made her own dolls and clothes but also designed and made clothes for other companies, which included: Horsman, Effanbee, Ideal, Sun Rubber (babies) Goldberger (My Fair Lady) & Cameo. She dressed Bye-Lo babies in long Christening clothes for Madame Hendren and at a later date made Bye-Lo babies, doll (composition) and clothes.

About 1937, she started Hollywood Cinema Fashions, dolls and clothes and designed such dolls and stars as: Irene Dunn, Jeannette McDonald, Deanna Durbin, Betty Grable, June Allison, Greer Garson, Oliva DeHaviland, Joan Crawford, June Depre as well as Queen Elizabeth, Princess Margaret Rose, Scarlett O'Hara and Melanie. She designed and had on the market a set of Little Women long before other manufacturers started promoting them. In 1940, there were six Glamour Girls (Movie Stars) on the market and even into the 1950's, using hard plastics, Mollye star dolls continued. And it must be remembered that all Shirley Temple clothes of 1933 and 1934 were tagged Mollye and she designed all Shirley Temple clothes to 1936 for Ideal Doll Co. Mollye dolls were displayed on the original Freedom Train after World War II.

After seeing the Thief of Bagdad, Mollye created an entire group of dolls to match the movie, including a Sabu, the little Indian boy of the movie but perhaps the most loved of all her creations was the Raggedy Ann and Andy whose registration dates March 1935, Patent No. 363008.

Johnny Gruelle, the author of the Raggedy series, and Mollye became good friends and invited Mollye and Myer to visit his home in Florida and then sent them on to Puerto Rico and Cartagena to visit other "toy people". Mollye had the patent to the Raggedy dolls when Mr. Gruelle died. She gave the rights to Mrs. Gruelle and in return, Mrs. Gruelle sold them to Knickerbocher Toy Co. The Supreme Court awarded Mollye the original faces when she did not want to sue.

To sum up Mollye Goldman would be hard but, in truth, it can be said, she is a beautiful lady, a successful lady with a sense of humor and a great amount of love, yes, love that suits Mollye! We will close this little salute to Mollye by telling you about one little thing that happened years ago: Mollye met a delightful young ventriloquist who asked her to design and make a wardrobe for his dummy. She did just that and the first outfit was a black tux. The vaudeville performer had moved on to another theatre in New York City and nearing completion of this first outfit, Mollye sent him a telegram and asked: "Does Charlie need a fly?" The answering telegram said, "Yes, of course Charlie needs a fly." signed Edgar Bergan.

These photos are all recent ones of Mollye Goldman, holding dolls that she has made and designed. Top, left to right: 18" "Peggy Rose Bride" 1939 & composition. All composition "Indian" and vinyl "Embassey Bride". Bottom row, left to right: A "Baby Joan", "Sabu", all composition from the Thief of Bagdad, 27" all composition Mexico.

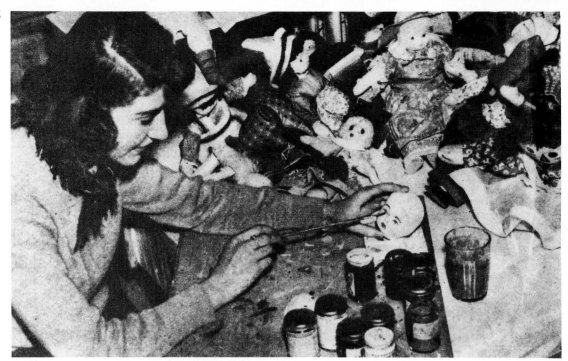

Above: How Mollye's dolls are born. Artist Juliet Fleche endows them with beauty in the Hollywood manner.

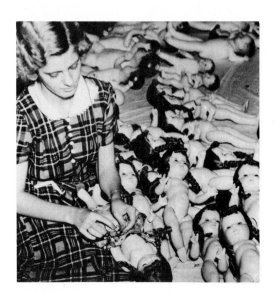

Mollye--This photo shows a group of all composition dolls having their wigs glued on at the Mollye factory. 1938.

Mollye--This is Mollye's niece "Snosh" in 1922 with a Mollye dressed doll. Cloth body with composition head and limbs. Snosh called the doll "Aunt Mollye".

Mollye--This is a Mollye photo of the first two International dolls created by Mollye in 1924. She used these dolls as her trademark.

Mollye--This is the Mollye designed and made "Beloved Belinda" that goes with the Mollye designed Raggedy Ann and Andy dolls. Size unknown. $95.00.

Mollye--24" "Muffin and Raggi-Muffin" Cloth with hand painted face masks and yarn hair. Made and designed by Mollye. 1931. $75.00 each.

Mollye--13'' ''Kate Greenaway'' 1928. All stuffed cloth with hand painted in oils, face. Yarn hair in sausage curls. Black silk tiered dress, rosette corsage at waist. Net inset at neck, lace mitt gloves & lace shawl. Matching bonnet with rosette trim. Shoulders and hips are stitch jointed. Pantaloons and slip are lace trimmed. $65.00.

Mollye--13½'' ''Carmela'' and ''Antonio'' of Italy. Pressed face, all cloth dolls by Mollye. Yarn hair. Jointed necks and stitched to be ''jointed'' at hips and shoulders. From International series. $55.00.

Mollye--13'' ''Little Louisa'' All cloth with yarn hair and hand painted features. Original clothes. Marks: A MOLLYE CREATION, on tag. $50.00.

Mollye--13'' ''Freida'' of Austria. All cloth with oil painted face mask. Original. Marks: Mollye DollOutfitters #2820, on tag. Made in U.S.A. Matching boy is named ''Otto''. $55.00. (Courtesy Edith DeAngelo)

Mollye--24" "Baby Joan" (Also called Baby Love) Cloth with pressed, hand painted in oils, face mask from England. $75.00.

Mollye--27" Deluxe "Spanish Girl" All cloth with oil painted face mask. Marks: None on doll. Mollye, on clothes tag. $125.00.

Mollye--27" "Mexico" & "Czech" Deluxe International. Cloth with imported face masks (England). Made from 1940 to 1958. Some have rejected parachutes with colors died in. These were made with rubber limbs, cloth bodies & composition heads also. $125.00.

Mollye--This photo shows the display of Mollye's clothes and dolls in 1935, at Gimbel Bros. department store. Rack holds Shirley Temple clothes, some dolls are Hollywood Cinema Fashions, Internationals and baby dolls.

Mollye--All toddlers and size ran from 14'' to 21''. All composition with sleep eyes. Three in back row are very chubby dolls. Circa 1935. Dolls most likely not marked, but clothes will be tagged Mollye. $35.00.

Mollye--Mollye Goldman designed the lamps and the clothes for a lamp maker during the early 1930's. This photo shows one of them. Lamp and clothes are unmarked. $32.00.

Mollye--24" "Dilly" All cloth with hand painted face features. Has Mollye tag sewn to bottom of foot. 1934. $65.00.

Mollye--16" "Snosh" All cloth with hand painted face on molded mask. Early 1930's. $45.00.

Mollye--29" "Sunny Girl" All cloth with molded, painted face mask. Note dark sateen used on arms. Original. Circa 1935. $65.00.

Mollye--24'' Mother (back row) called "Sherry Ann" and 15'' daughter, "Cindy Ann''. Front row is the "Dee" Family. Left to right: 21'' "Lilly Dee", 18'' "Daisy Dee'' and 15'' "Twinkle Dee". All the dolls are composition. 1944-45. 15'' $65.00. 18'' $85.00. 21'' $100.00. 24'' $125.00.

Mollye--15" "French" All composition with sleep eyes and human hair wig. Original.
Marks: None on doll. "Mollye Creations", on gown tag. 1938. $125.00.

Mollye--All these dolls are all composition and of the mid-1930's. All are originally dressed and designed (clothes by Mollye). The quality of the clothes, as well as the design is most exceptional.

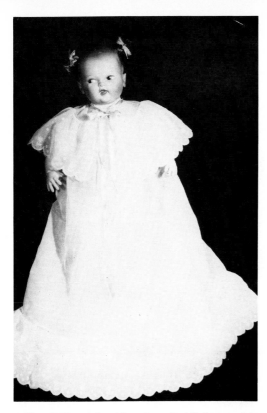

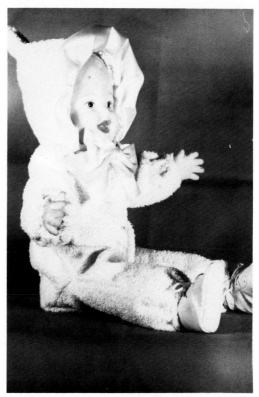

Mollye--14" "Baby First Born" All latex with jointed neck only. Painted eyes to side and has two holes in head for tuffs of hair. Original gown designed by Mollye. $35.00.

Mollye--19" "Terrykins" Vinyl head with painted eyes and open/closed mouth. One piece latex body & limbs. Terry cloth outfit.

Mollye--17" "Business Girl" All hard plastic with special styled wig and clothes designed by Mollye. All original. Sleep blue eyes. Marks: None. 1952. $75.00.

Mollye--36" "Polly Ann" Plastic and vinyl with white rooted hair. Blue sleep eyes. Marks: None on doll. Mollye clothes, on tag. All original. 1961. $85.00.

Mollye--This is the photo at the Toy Fair about 1950. The dolls have hard plastic heads (babies) and cloth bodies with latex limbs. The small dolls are all hard plastic with one piece body and legs and painted on shoes.

Mollye--This is a department store display of Mollye items, both dolls and clothes. All the dolls are all composition. The 9'' all composition baby called ''Angel'' is on the left. Lower left case holds Shirley Temple clothes. 1934.

Mollye--These International dolls were featured on the original Freedom Train after
W.W.II. Mollye began making these dolls in 1924. She made both the dolls and designed and made all the clothes. All will have tags saying Mollye Creations.

Mollye--27'' ''Jeanette McDonald'' All composition (has long neck) with long thin limbs and torso. Sleep greenish eyes/lashes. Open mouth/four teeth. One arm is slightly bent. Marks: None. The inset shows Jeanette McDonald, along with Nelson Eddy from their film ''Maytime''. $350.00. (Courtesy Diane Duster)

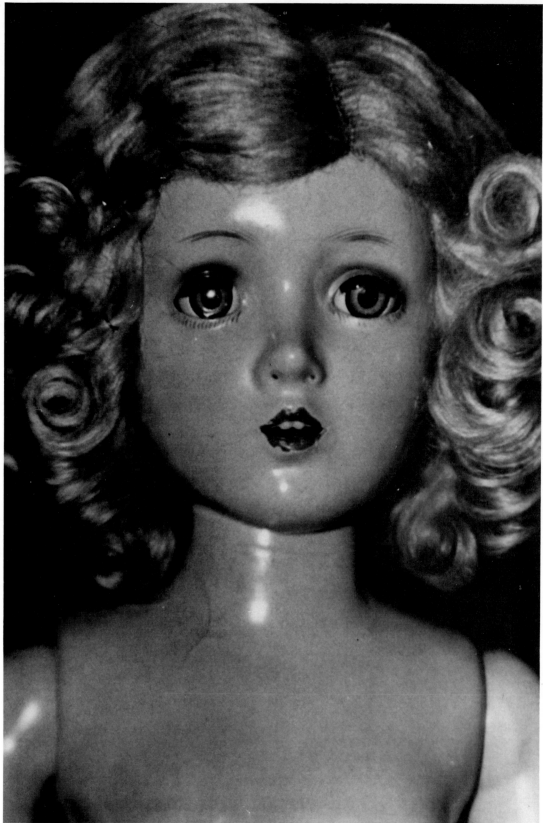

Mollye--This is a close-up of the all composition
"Jeanette McDonald" doll. (Courtesy Diane
Duster)

Mollye--This is the Thief of Bagdad group of dolls made by Mollye and each is a work of art! T he men's faces, clothes, and beards were all designed and made by Mollye. All the dolls are 14'' to 19'' tall, and of high grade composition. Some have cloth bodies.

Mollye--19'' ''Sultan'' from the picture, The Thief of Bagdad. Satin coat is purple. Features hand painted in oils. All made and designed by Mollye. $200.00.

Mollye--36" "Bru" This doll was bought in Paris by Mr. Maurice Stern of Bloom-ingdales Dept. Store in 1934. Mollye was invited to lunch with Mr. Stern and was told that bacause she was the preferred source for dolls & clothes for the American Merchan-dise Corp and supplied dolls and clothes to such stores as Strawbridge, Clother, L. Hudson, Heebe, Marshall Fields and many other fine department stores, and that he (Mr. Stern) had been sent to Europe to buy dolls and wanted Mollye to dress them, which she did. Mollye purchased this doll (Bru) from Mr. Stern. It was sold to an anti-que dealer some years ago and later sold at the Park, Bennet Gallery. The doll is dressed as June Deprey the leading lady of the Thief of Bagdad. Mollye designed clothing and bed.

Mollye--This photo shows "Sabu", the leading star of the movie, The Thief of Bagdad showing Mrs. Arthur Goldsmith, President of the doll club (N.Y.), Mrs. Virginia Muggley and Mollye Goldman (center). Mrs. Muggley worked for Mollye for 22 years. Mollye sculptured the first head of Sabu at the Y.M.C.A. in Philadelphia. Here Sabu is showing how to wind a turban. Doll - $175.00.

Mollye--15'' 1940 Glamour Girl ''Ginger Rogers''
All composition with sleep eyes/lashes. Gown is
light green taffeta with plaid silk taffeta underskirt of red/green and gold. Human hair wig.
$185.00.

Mollye--20'' ''Society Deb'' All composition in silk taffeta gown. Hand painted face and hand made jewelry. Marks: None. 1939. $100.00.

Mollye--9'' ''Martha Washington'' All hard plastic with one piece body and legs. hand painted faces. White mohair wig. Original. $5.00.

Mollye--27" "Pamela" Bride of 1939. All composition with attached cloth busts. Human hair wig, sleep eyes/lashes and open mouth. Marks: None. $125.00.

Mollye--12" "Perkett" All vinyl with rooted hair, sleep eyes/lashes. Marks: Molly 'E, on head. $15.00.

Mollye--15" "Spanish Lady" Plastic with vinyl arms and head. Sleep eyes/lashes, and slightly smiling mouth. Marks: Molly-'es, on head. $18.00.

Mollye--28" "Buzzy" Hard plastic head with sleep eyes/lashes and molded hair. Cloth body with latex arms and legs. Original. Marks: None. $45.00.

Mollye--Mollye dressed dolls for the Effanbee Company during the 1930's. This is a Patsy Ann dressed by her in 1939. The dress is pink with small flowers, blue satin tie and ruffled collar. Doll is all composition. Marks: Effanbee/"Patsy Ann"/Pat. 1283558, on back. $85.00. (Courtesy Edith DeAngelo)

Mollye--This is a photo of the Patsy Ann (Effanbee) with coat and hat on over pink dress in other picture. Real fur trim. Designed and made by Mollye for Effanbee. (Courtesy Edith DeAngelo)

Mollye--23" Hard plastic walker. Blue sleep eyes. Open mouth with four teeth & felt tongue. Red saran wig, beautifully done with hair net. Very detailed bridal outfit including hoop slip, lace trimmed veil, and trimmed nylon skirt over taffeta dress. Socks and white satin snap shoes. Ring of felt and paper flowers for headpiece. Bouquet of net, flowers and streaming ribbon. Marks: None. $65.00. (Courtesy Austin Collection)

Mollye--20" "Mamie Eisenhower" with special wig glued on. Doll is hard plastic with vinyl head. Open/closed mouth, sleep eyes/lashes. Marks: X, in circle on head. Was on music box stand. $125.00.

Mollye--14'' "Judy Garland" All composition. Blue tin sleep eyes with feathered lashes above the eyes. No eyebrows. Marks: None on doll. A MOLLYE'S PRODUCT/AMERICAN MADE, on dress tag. Came in 14'', 16'' and 21''. $125.00

Mollye--Shows original clothes on the 14'' Judy Garland. Wig is dark brown mohair in original set. Shoes and socks are replaced.

Mollye--This is photo of the especially designed Mollye music box. The base is white with on and off switch & no wind up key. The doll's feet slide into the bands on the top. $15.00.

Mollye--Shows sheet that came with the extra Mollye made and designed clothes for dolls.

Mollye--19'' ''Dancing Deb'' Hard plastic with vinyl head and glued on wig. Stands on revolving music box. Sleep eyes/lashes. Open/closed mouth. Marks: X, in a circle, on head. $85.00.

Mollye--19'' ''Embassy Bride'' Hard plastic with vinyl head, glued on wig, sleep eyes/lashes. Originally was on a music box that as it played, revolved the doll. Marks: X, in circle, on head. $85.00. (Courtesy Phyllis Houston)

Mollye--This is the Embassey Bride undressed and shows the attached ''falsies'' and close-up of head marked with an X, in a circle. This head is identical to one used by Alexander Doll Co. for two years. (Courtesy Phyllis Houston)

Mollye--This is the leg of the Embassey Bride to show the detail Mollye put into her dolls. The stocking is set with rhinestones and she has a garter. (Courtesy Phyllis Houston)

Mollye--19'' ''Betty Grable'' Hard plastic with vinyl head and white wig. Gown is pink with swirls. Wears heart necklace. Stands on revolving music box. This same doll was also used as Dancing Deb. $125.00. (Courtesy Edith DeAngelo)

211

Mollye--19" "Princess Margaret Rose" Hard plastic with vinyl head. Sleep eyes/lashes. Open/closed mouth. Gown is white and she wears a gold tiara. $135.00. (Courtesy Edith DeAngelo)

Mollye--29" "Mexican Girl" Cloth body with composition head and limbs. 1944. Part of clothing is made from unused parachutes. Marks: None on doll. International Doll Co. Phil. Pa./Created by Mollye, on box. $185.00. (Courtesy Edith DeAngelo)

Mollye--19" Olivia DeHaviland as "Melanie" from Gone With The Wind. Hard plastic with vinyl head. Sleep eyes/lashes. Open/closed mouth. Glued on wig. Some of these dolls are marked with an X in a circle. $195.00. (Courtesy Edith DeAngelo)

Mollye--19" "Princess Elizabeth Rose" Hard plastic and vinyl head with sleep eyes/lashes. Open/closed mouth. All original bride. Marks: X, in a circle on head. $165.00. (Courtesy Edith DeAngelo)

Mollye--This photo shows Mayor Bernard Samuels of Philadelphia and President of American Airlines with the Mollye Airlines Stewardess doll.

Mollye--This shows an original "Chris", the American Airlines Stewardess doll in case. She is all hard plastic with sleep eyes. The doll came in sizes 14'', 18'', 23'' and 28''. Promoted by Jane Wyman in the movie "Three Guys Named Mike". $95.00.

Mollye--20" "Margaret Rose Bride" and also "Embassy Bride" Vinyl head with hard
plastic body. Sleep eyes/lashes. Open/closed mouth. Marks: X, in circle on head.
Stands on revolving music box. $85.00.

Mollye--9" "Swedish Girl" All vinyl with sleep eyes and rooted hair. Marks: Molye-E, on head. $15.00. (Courtesy Edith DeAngelo)

Mollye--17" All composition with brown sleep eyes/lashes. Closed mouth. Pink pin dotted or organdie dress with lace trim. One piece lace trimmed underclothes. Pink side snap shoes with buckle/bow. Pink ribbon rosette tie. Human hair wig in Page Boy style. Marks: None on doll. A Mollye-E'S/Product/American Made, on tag.$125.00.

Mollye--19" "Regal Bride" All hard plastic with large blue sleep eyes with lashes painted on beneath the eyes. Glued on wig, palms turned to body. Open mouth with teeth and tongue. Original, minus veil. Marks: None. $65.00. (Courtesy Jena Durham)

Mollye--18" This is a basic doll that Mollye used for several personalities. All hard plastic with glued on blonde hair. Sleep blue eyes/lashes. Open mouth/four teeth. Felt tongue. 1953. Marks: 200, on head.

Mollye--13" "341 Dream Baby" (Armand Marseilles) with closed mouth. Bisque head with composition baby body. Dressed by Mollye for F.A.O. Schwartz. About 1921. Mollye dressed many bisque headed dolls for different department stores. $285.00. (Courtesy Edith DeAngelo)

Mollye--13" "Rudi, the Swiss Lad" #2841 (18" size is #1841) Marks: None on doll. A Mollye Doll/Copyright 1938, on tag. Mollye made 28 different International Dolls, both boys and girls. $45.00. (Courtesy Edith DeAngelo)

Mollye--8½" All vinyl "Tyrolean Girl" 1958. Marks: Mollye, on head. Sleep blue eyes. Excellent quality clothes. $15.00.

Mollye--8½" "Scots Lass" Plastic and vinyl with blue sleep eyes. Excellent quality clothing. Marks: MOLLYE, on head. CREATED/BY/MOLLYE, on tag. $15.00.

Mollye--21'' ''Baby Joan'' Long cloth body with latex limbs. Hard plastic heads with open mouth/2 upper teeth. Sleep eyes/lashes. Marks: 450, on head of blonde. None, on red head. Both are original. $35.00.

Mollye--15'' ''Swedish Girl'' Plastic body with vinyl head and arms. Sleep blue eyes/lashes and closed, slightly smiling, mouth. Original. Marks: None. Came in a window box.

Mollye--21'' ''Baby Joan'' Long cloth body with latex limbs. Hard plastic heads with open mouth/2 upper teeth. Sleep eyes/lashes. Marks: 450, on head of blonde. None, on red head. Both are original. $35.00.

Mollye--15'' ''Cynthia'' One piece stuffed vinyl body & limbs. Jointed neck. Vinyl head with big, deep blue sleep eyes. Rooted hair. Open/closed mouth. An original dress. Marks: 15, on head. ''V'', low on back. $35.00. (Courtesy Phyllis Houston)

Mollye--1935 infant and toddler doll garment by Mollye. $10.00.

Mollye--An original packaged baby dress by Hollywood Cinema Creations by Mollye. $10.00.

Mollye--These are three of the different pressed faces that Mollye had made exclusively for her in England.

Miner Industries--14" "Suntan Suzy" All rigid vinyl with orange tones. High heel feet, painted nails and sleep blue eyes. Rooted dark hair and young adult busts. Has U.S. Pat. No. 2,921,407. Put her in the sun and she darkens and after being inside for awhile she turns to natural shade. Marks: H, on head. 15 BAL HH, on back. $12.00. (Courtesy Phyllis Houston)

Merry--4-1/8" "Jodi" All vinyl with painted black hair and brown eyes. Fully jointed. Made by Merry Mfg. Co. 1966. $3.00. (Courtesy Phyllis Houston)

NANCY ANN STORYBOOK DOLLS
Nancy Ann Abbott began making doll in 1942 and at it's peak put out over eight thousand dolls a day. Nancy Ann Storybook Dolls, unless found with their wrists tag/box, are unidentifiable. She has made dolls of painted bisque, all hard plastic and later in vinyl. In 1952 Muffie, and 7-8" doll was born, who had an extensive wardrobe and became very popular. Baby and Black Nancy Ann dolls are considered rare.

Nancy Ann Storybook--5½" "Bridesmaid Teen" #87. All painted bisque. $12.00. (Courtesy Anita Pacey)

Nancy Ann Storybook--5½" "First Confirmation" All hard plastic. Glued on blonde mohair wig. Fully jointed. Sleep eyes. Painted on shoes and gloves. Original white nylon dress and veil, prayerbook. $12.00. (Courtesy Phyllis Houston)

Nancy Ann Storybook--5½" "Friday's Child" All painted bisque. Marks: None on doll. Friday's Child Is Loving and Giving, on tag. #184. $12.00. (Courtesy Anita Pacey)

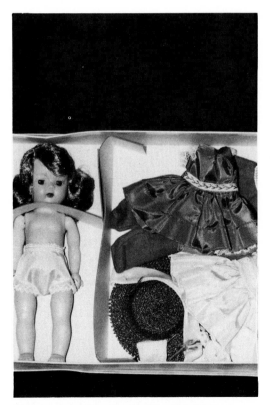

Nancy Ann Storybook--6½" Dressed in white satin with blue flowers. Pale blue picture hat. Sleep black eyes. All plastic. Marks: Storybook/Dolls.U.S.A./Trademark/Reg, on back. $12.00. (Courtesy Kathleen Flowers Council)

Nancy Ann Storybook--8" "Muffie" in an original box. 1953. All hard plastic. $15.00. (Courtesy Marge Meisinger)

Nancy Ann Storybook--6¼" Painted bisque with peach taffeta dress. Blue felt hat with blue flowers and peach ribbon. White lace umbrella with peach ribbon and pipe cleaner handle. Marks: A Show Girl For April 190, on box. 190 April Girl, on wrist tag. $12.00. (Courtesy Evelyn Chisman)

Nancy Ann Storybook--5½" "One Two-Button My Shoe" #123. Marked on box and wrist tag. Painted bisque. Red felt hat with white feather. Red dress top with red/green/white plaid skirt. Painted black shoes with three buttons. Marks: Storybook Doll/USA/Pat App. for. $12.00. (Courtesy Evelyn Chisman)

Nancy Ann Storybook--5½" "Red Riding Hood" #116, marked both on box and wrist tag. Painted bisque with plastic hood and cape. White dress tied with red ribbon. Marks: Story Book/Doll/USA/Pat/App/For. $12.00. (Courtesy Evelyn Chisman)

Nancy Ann Storybook--7" "Angel" Painted bisque. The angel wings are plastic trimmed in silver. Pipe cleaner wand with silver star. $12.00. (Courtesy Evelyn Chisman)

Nancy Ann Storybook--5½" "Bridesmaid" #87 from the Family Series. Marked both on box and wrist tag. Painted bisque. Light lavender satin dress with lace trim & pink ribbon at waist. Cap is lace with pink ribbon. Unusual mark on doll: Nancy/Ann/Storybook/Dolls. $12.00. (Courtesy Evelyn Chisman)

Nancy Ann Storybook--5½" "Western Miss" Pink checked cotton dress & bonnet. Attached white apron. Painted bisque. Marks: 58 Western Miss, on wrist tag. American Girl Series/Western Miss/58. $12.00. (Courtesy Evelyn Chisman)

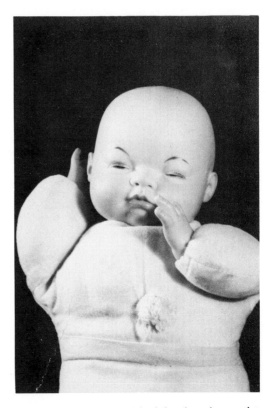

Nancy Ann Storybook--7" "Muffie" as India. This doll was made in 1968, one of the re-issued series, taken from the old mold and made from the same good quality hard plastic. Painted red dot on forehead. Walker, head turns. Marks: None. $8.00. (Courtesy Yvonne Baird)

Nasco--18" "Sleepy" Vinyl head and gauntlet hands and stuffed cloth body. Painted eyes are mere slits. Marks: NASCO/1960. $12.00. (Courtesy Phyllis Houston)

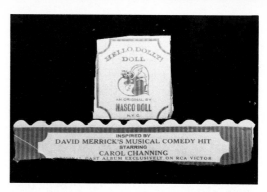

Nasco--Shows the box information in the Hello Dolly Doll.

Nasco--24" "Hello Dolly", Carol Channing. Plastic with vinyl head. Sleep blue eyes/lashes. High heels. Original. Blue-grey eyeshadow. Marks: 1373/K/1961. Rooted white hair. See following photo information on box. $165.00.

Nasco--7½" "Colonial Belles" Plastic body with vinyl head & limbs. Sleep blue eyes/lashes. Six in set. Marks: MADE IN/TAIWAN, on back. BY NASCO, on box. 1975. $4.00.

Natural--13" "Ritzy Chubby Baby" All composition with one piece body and head. Painted blue eyes. Dimples. Mohair wig over molded hair. Marks: None, on doll. It's a Natural/Ritzy Chubby Baby Dolls/Natural Doll Co. Inc./Est. 1915/Made/In/ U.S.A., on tag. Circa 1937. $16.00. (Courtesy Barbara Monzelluzzi)

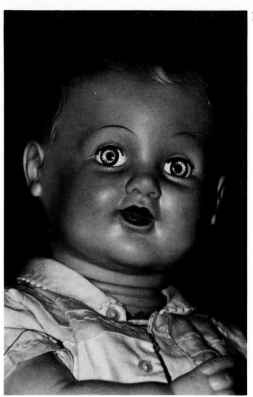

Natural--16½'' ''Bride'' Hard plastic walker with sleep eyes and open mouth. Marks: None. Original. 1952. $15.00. (Courtesy Anita Pacey)

Natural--18'' ''Pitter-Pat'' All vinyl with stuffed vinyl head. Sleep blue eyes/heavy lashes. Open/closed mouth. Beautiful ear detail. Marks: None. 1954. $8.00.

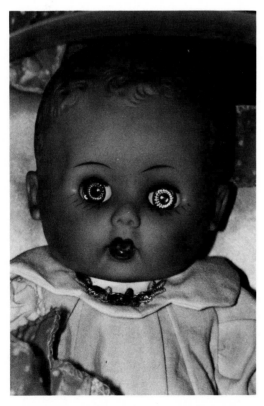

Natural--11'' ''Natural Baby'' All vinyl and of good quality. Blue sleep eyes/lashes. Open mouth/nurser. Marks: 3-R, on head. Original. 1957. $6.00. (Courtesy Anita Pacey)

Natural--Shows the 11'' all vinyl baby in original basket. (Courtesy Anita Pacey)

NEW YORK TOY & GAME--6" "Junior W.A.A.C." All composition doll that is jointed at the shoulders only. Sewing set and shown with box top. Marks: New York Toy & Game/Mfg. Co. 12 E 22nd/N.Y., N.Y., on box. 1943. $12.00. (Photo courtesy Carolyn Powers)

Natural-- 10½" "Little Netty" All vinyl with very dark molded hair. Blue sleep eyes. Open mouth/nurser. Marks: 1008/AE/14. $5.00. (Courtesy Phyllis Houston)

Pam Toys--18" "Baby Rock A Bye" Key wind, doll rocks baby and closes eyes. All plastic with vinyl heads. Baby is 6½". Marks: Pam Toys, on head of baby. Made in Hong Kong, on back of girl. Copy of far better quality Italian doll. 1976. Still available. (Courtesy Anita Pacey)

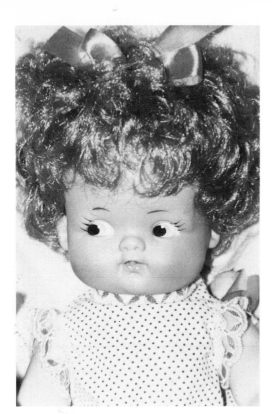

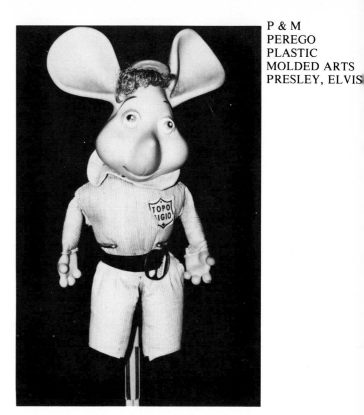

P & M Doll Co.--12" "Little Miss Mary" & "Baby Buttons" Plastic and vinyl with painted blue eyes to the side. Open mouth/nurser. Original. 1968. Marks: None on doll. P & M Doll Co. Little Miss Mary, on box. $4.00. (Courtesy Anita Pacey)

Perego--13" "Topo Gigio" Cloth with vinyl head. Vinyl hands. Rooted hair. Marks: 1963/Maria Perego, on head. $7.00. (Courtesy Kimport Dolls)

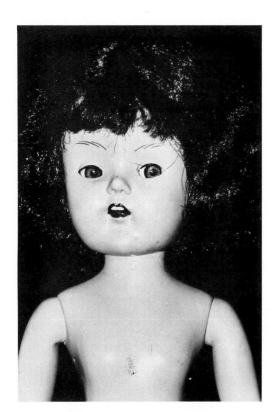

Plastic Molded Arts--15" "Jenny Walker" All hard plastic with flirty sleep green eyes. Open mouth/two upper teeth. Walker, head turns. Marks: PLASTIC MOLDED ARTS CO./L.I.C. NEW YORK, on back. 1953. $6.00.

Elvis Presley--18" "Elvis Presley" This ad is from the magazine "Hep Cats" of Dec. 1956 and was loaned to us by an avid Elvis collector, Sue Demerly. The ad states: Doll that looks just like Elvis, gyrates like Elvis. It is not known if doll is just jointed at the waist or battery operated. It has been reported that the doll is marked: Elvis Presley Enterprises 1957. (Courtesy Sue Demerly)

227

Puppet--4'' Tall head of plaster with deeply mold-ed hair and hand painted. Plastic feet and arms. Marks: Copyright 1949 A.C. Graebner/ Marionette Parts/National Supply Service Boy Scouts of America/Cat. No. 1897A, on box. A.C. Graebner, on head. $6.00. (Courtesy Joan Amundsen)

Puppet--10'' ''Mary'' Vinyl head with black molded hair. Large painted blue eyes to side. Molded blue hair ribbons. Marks: Mary from Babe in Toyland/Copyright Walt Disney Prod./ Gund Mfg. Co. $5.00. (Courtesy Marie Ernst)

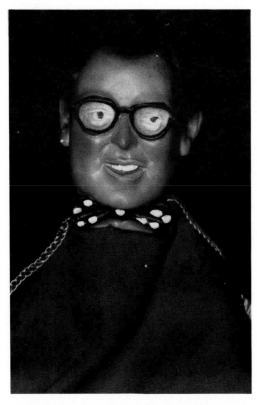

Puppet--9'' ''Clark Kent'' (Superman) hand pup-pet with vinyl head and cotton hand mitt. Marks: None. $3.00. (Courtesy Joan Amundsen)

Puppet--10'' Hand puppet with vinyl head and plastic hand mitt. Red yarn hair with separate hat that is glued on. Marks: Remco/1970, on head. $3.00.

Puppets--12" "Bozo, The Capitol Clown" Cloth body and arms with felt hands. Talk box in body. Pull string operated. Vinyl head with rooted orange yarn hair. Painted features. Marks: MATTEL/BOZO THE CAPITOL CLOWN/ CAPITOL RECORDS, INC./1963, on tag. $4.00.

Puppet--12" "King Kong" & 3" "Bobby Bond" Cloth with vinyl head and talking mechanism. Hand puppet. Bobby Bond is all one piece vinyl. Held with a strip of tape. Marks: HK, on head. 1966/RKO GENERAL INC. Mattel, on tag. $4.00.

Puppet--10" Talking hand puppet with the Wizard of Oz characters. 1967. $8.00. (Courtesy Phyllis Houston)

Puppet--"Monkies" Talking hand puppet by Mattel with portraits of the four singers. 1967. $12.00. (Courtesy Phyllis Houston)

Puppet--12" Cloth & vinyl. Painted features. Pull string talker. Marks: MATTEL/CHAR. 1950 ROBERT E (BOB) CLAMPETT/MATTEL VOICE UNIT US PAT. 3,017,187, on tag. $2.00.

Puppet--10" "Snow Queen" Hand puppet with vinyl head and plastic hand covering. Marks: None. $2.00. (Courtesy Phyllis Houston)

Puppet--16" "Blue Fairy" Plastic and wood with movable mouth. Marks: HAZELLETE MARIONETTE/ MADE IN KANSAS CITY, MO., on tag. Talker. 1958. $6.00.

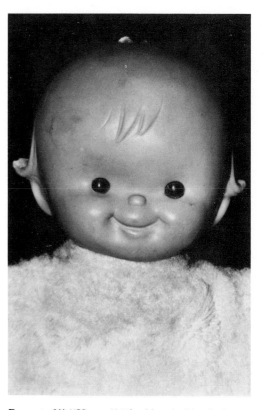

Puppet--9" "Happy" Vinyl head with plush mitt. Painted features. Molded tuffs of blonde hair. Marks: HAPPY/1965/ELKA TOY. $2.00. (Courtesy Pearl Clasby)

Remco--5½" "Sweet April" All original. Plastic body with vinyl head and limbs. Inset eyes. Open mouth/nurser. Button in back makes arm move. Marks: REMCO IND. INC./1972. Has tear ducts. Came with many accessories. $6.00. (Courtesy Phyllis Houston)

Richard Toy Co.--11½" "Little Girl Pink" and "Little Boy Blue" He has freckles. Both have brown sleep eyes. Closed puckered mouths. Fingers spread. Flat feet. He's in blue and she's in pink. Marks: MADE IN HONG KONG, on heads. RICHARD TOY CO. LTD, on box. 1974. $4.00. (Courtesy Phyllis Houston)

Roy Design--6" "Clown" All rigid vinyl with inset mohair. Painted features. Cut in back for bank. Marks: ROY DES. OF FLORIDA. $2.00. (Courtesy Virginia Jones)

Roy Design--8" "Moose" All rigid vinyl with painted features. Felt clothes and tongue. hole in back for bank. Marks: ROY DES. OF FLORIDA. $2.00. (Courtesy Virginia Jones)

Royal--19½'' ''Lilo'' 1958. All vinyl with jointed waist. Almost black rooted hair. Green sleep eyes/lashes. High heels & red fingernails. Was released in England as Elizabeth Taylor. Marks: Royal Doll, (some) on head. Original. $22.00.

Royal--15'' ''Debbie'' Excellent vinyl with jointed elbows. Doll is strung. Open mouth. Dimples. Sleep blue eyes/lashes. Marks: ROYAL DOLL, on back. ROYAL DOLL/1961, on head. $18.00.

Royal--12'' ''Jodi'' Plastic body with head & limbs of vinyl. Open mouth/nurser. Sleep blue eyes/lashes. Bent baby legs. Marks: 1964/Royal Doll/10. $16.00.

Royal--12'' ''Merry Lee'' Good quality vinyl with molded hair. Open mouth with no wetting hole in body. Sleep blue eyes/lashes. Marks: Royal Doll Co./1964. $12.00.

Royal--12" "Joy Bride" Shown with Joy that has tag missing. The dress is lavender/blue and grey. Both designed by Miss Rose of Royal Doll Co. Marks: A Royal Doll/1965. $20.00. (Courtesy Anita Pacey)

Royal--12" "Joy in France" In blue with white bodice, pinafore with blue trim. Other Joy has missing tag. Dress is dark grey with white eyelet apron and white collar. Both are 1965. $20.00. (Courtesy Anita Pacey)

Royal--12" "Joy" a Puritan in dark blue with white apron and collar and Joy in Germany. Red with white bodice, white apron and trim. 1965. $20.00. (Courtesy Anita Pacey)

Shindana--16" "Dee Bee" All cloth with vinyl hands and head. Painted eyes. Front left: 11" "Lea" All foam covered with vinyl hands and head. Painted eyes. Non-removable clothes. $6.00. Front right: 11" "Li'l Soft Soul" All one piece poly-foam. Jointed neck only. $6.00. (Courtesy 1975 Shindana Catalog)

Shindana--22" "Kesha" Foam filled cloth body. Vinyl arms, legs and head. Sleep eyes. Marks: SHINDANA/Operations Bootstrap/1974. $12.00.

Shindana--16" "Tamu" (NEW) & 16-3/4" "Rodney Allen Rippy". Tamu: Pull string talker, says: Pick me up, Hold me tight, etc. All cloth with vinyl hands and head. Painted eyes. Rodney: Pull string talker. Says 10 different things. All printed cloth. Tamu $9.00 and Rodney $16.00.

Shindana--16" "Lisa" All cloth with vinyl head. Comes in two hair styles. hands are "Velcro" which permits the doll to hold things. Comes with pad, and crayon so doll can learn to write along with the child. $10.00. (Courtesy Shindana 1975 catalog)

Sayco--20" "Pouty Paul" Plastic body & legs. Vinyl head & arms. Sleep blue eyes. Marks: SAYCO/DOLL CORP N.Y.C. 1964. Refer to Series 11-page 296 for another version of this same doll. This is a toddler body with a cryer in the stomach. $10.00. (Courtesy Bessie Carson)

Shimmel Sons--9" "Betty Boop" Plastic with vinyl head. Marks: Hong Kong, on back. King Features/Syndicates Inc. MSS/M. Shimmel/Sons/Inc./#9123. 1976-77. $6.00.

Sonsco--14" "Bonnie Dee" Plastic with vinyl head. Push button, battery operated talker. Sleep cobalt blue eyes/lashes. Original. Marks: None. 1973. $8.00. (Courtesy Anita Pacey)

Squeeze Toy--7" All vinyl. Marks: IDEAL TOY CORP/MUM-1. HANNA BARBERA PROD. INC. $2.00.

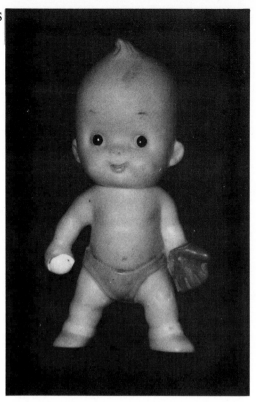

Squeeze Toys--4" All vinyl with jointed neck. Molded on baseball and mitt. Painted eyes. Marks: C, on head. JAPAN/C, on back. $2.00. (Courtesy Marie Ernst)

Squeeze Toys--6½" "Wimpy" All vinyl. Marks: KING FEATURES/SYNDICATE. $4.00. (Courtesy Virginia Jones)

Squeeze Toys--9" "Bucky Bradford" of the Grant's Bradford House restaurants. One piece vinyl. $3.00. (Courtesy Virgina Jones)

Squeeze Toys--8" "Cindy" All vinyl. Marks: 22/ THE EDWARD MOBERLY CO., on head. THE EDWARD MOBERLY CO/MFG BY THE AR-ROW RUBBER AND PLASTIC CORP. 27/1962. $2.00.

Squeeze Toys--10" "Baby Hewie" All vinyl. Marks: HARVEY. $2.00.

Squeeze Toys--8" "Buck" All vinyl. Molded clothes. Painted features. Marks: None, on doll. BUCK/SOFT STANDING/SCENTED/VINYL DOLL MFG BY STAHLWOOD TOY MFG. CO. INC., on box. 1955. $2.00.

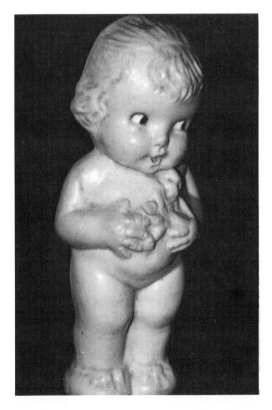

Squeeze Toys--5½" All one piece vinyl. Holding doll. Marks: IRWIN, on back. $2.00.

Squeeze Toys--5" "Frog" All vinyl. Marks: JE McCONNELL. $1.00.

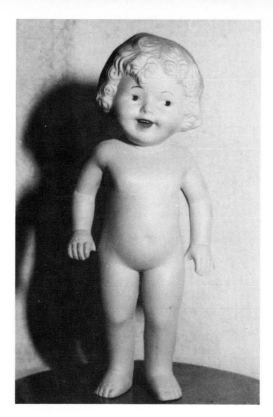

Suni Toy--14" "Little Lulu" Inflatable doll. Marks: Suni Toy, in oval/200 Fifth Ave./New York N.Y./1973/Western Publishing Company Inc./No. 1106/Made in Taiwan. $2.00.

Sun Rubber--7½" "Little Natalia" All one piece rubber with painted features and Shirley Temple style hairdo. Open/closed smiling mouth. Marks: Little Natalia/Sun Rubber Co., etc. $35.00. (Photo courtesy Loretta Zablotny)

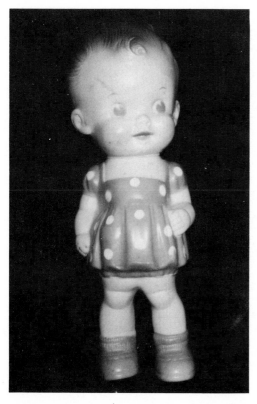

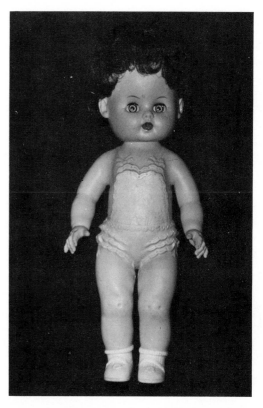

Sun Rubber--8½" "Dotty" All vinyl with molded brown hair. Painted blue eyes. Open/closed mouth with molded tongue. Jointed neck. Molded on dress, shoes and socks. Marks: RUTH E NEWTON/THE SUN RUBBER CO, on head. RUTH E NEWTON/THE SUN RUBBER CO, on body. 1955. $2.00.

Sun Rubber--13" "Sun Dee" On one piece vinyl body with molded on rompers, shoes and socks. Sleep blue eyes. Open mouth/nurser with no hole in body. Marks: SUN DEE/THE SUN RUBBER CO. 1956/BARBERTON, OHIO. $6.00. (Courtesy Marie Ernst)

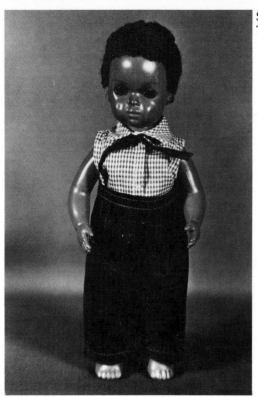

Sunshine--14" "Happy" A Sunshine Doll. Drink and wet, sleep eyes, rooted hair, original dress and fully jointed. Body is almost perfectly round. Marks: 19(C)64, on back. $6.00. (Courtesy Phyllis Houston)

Terri Lee--10" "Benji" (Tiny Jerri Lee) Lamb's wool wig and sleep brown eyes. Walker. Tagged clothes. $65.00.

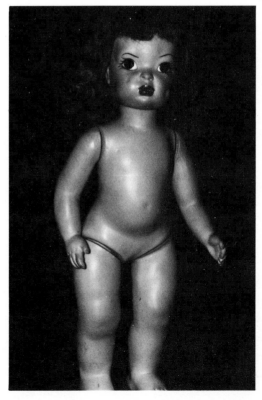

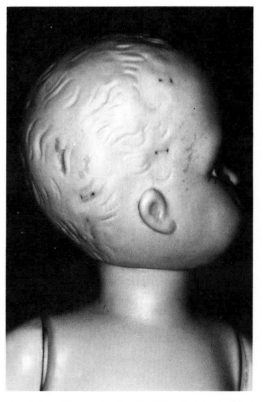

Terri Lee--15½" "Terri Lee" All "Lastic-Plastic" (Early Vinyl). Slightly molded hair under wig. Excellent toe and fingernail detail. Marks: None. $85.00.

Terri Lee--Shows the detail of the slightly molded hair under the wig of the vinyl Terri Lee.

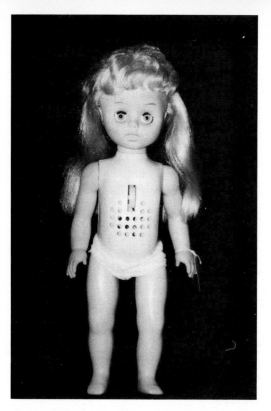

Thomas Premiums--7" "Happy Mouth Bottle Opener" (Portrait of Jimmy Carter). Wood handle with metal bottle opener inside vinyl head with wide open mouth. Opening in back allows emptying caps. Marks: Thomas Premiums Ltd. 1976/Made in Japan, on box. $10.00.

Tomy--14" Plastic with vinyl arms & head. Sleep blue eyes/lashes. Open/closed mouth. Battery operated talker with start button in chest. Hair styled in side pony tails. Marks: TOMY/PAT. P. 79108535-24065/25767-32829/U.K. Pat. P 50385/MADE IN HONG KONG. $4.00. (Courtesy Marie Ernst)

Toy Product--12½" "Lil Sis" Very early crude composition. Painted eyes and hair. Original dress. Marks: LIL SIS/A /TOY PRODUCT. 1933. $5.00. (Courtesy Phyllis Houston)

Trolls--5½" All original with felt clothing and leather shield. Charteuse hair and blue eyes. Marks: Dam Thing, in a circle on back. 1965. $3.00. (Courtesy Phyllis Houston)

Trolls--3'' ''Trolls'' All vinyl and jointed at neck only. Unmarked but have a protuded bump at base of neck that was used to punch a hole in and to hang the troll from a string. $3.00.

Trolls--3'' ''Hawaiian Troll'' All vinyl. Marks: '64, on back. $3.00. (Courtesy Eileeen Harris)

Trolls--3'' ''Sock It To Me Troll'' from ''Laugh In'' T.V. program. This is one of the ''Wish-niks'' series. Has painted black eye. Marks: Uneeda/Wish-nik. $3.00. (Courtesy Eileen Harris)

Trolls--3'' ''Monster Troll'' These all vinyl trolls are unmarked. Originally had black one piece outfit on. $4.00. (Courtesy Eileen Harris).

10" "Suzette" All vinyl. Three painted lashes as well as molded ones. Marks: Suzy's teenage sister, on box. Made by Uneeda but uses the circle X or circle P mold. Uneeda, marked on head. $6.00. (Courtesy Virginia Jones)

Uneeda--16½" "Chubby Toddler" Plastic and vinyl head. Has dimples and closed mouth. Sleep blue eyes. Original. Marks: Uneeda/3, on head. $6.00. (Courtesy Anita Pacey)

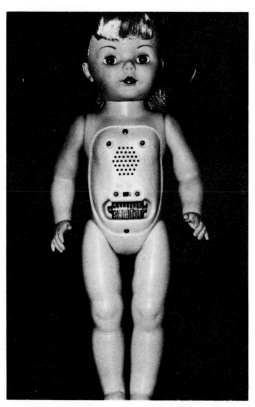

Uneeda--21" "Sarenade" Plastic body and legs. Battery operated talker. Vinyl arms and head. Sleep blue eyes/lashes. Smile closed mouth with dimples. Rooted ponytail. Marks: Uneeda/Doll Co. Inc./1962. $12.00.

Uneeda--18" "Little Coquette" Toddlers with same bodies. Plastic with vinyl heads. Sleep blue eyes/lashes. Wide open mouth/nursers. All fingers on left hand are curled with extended thumbs. Left: Slight dimples below eyes. Marks: Uneeda/Doll/Inc., in circle/1963/17/N.F. Right doll has wider face and cheek dimples, plus oval eyes. Marks: Uneeda/Dolls/inc./MDMLXX-lll/1873Y. $6.00.

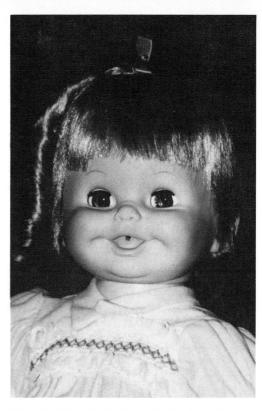

Uneeda--17" "Tammy" All vinyl, excellent quality girl with red rooted hair in original set, blue sleep eyes, tiny dimples by mouth. Clothes are also original. Marks: (C)/UNEEDA, on neck. $8.00. (Courtesy Phyllis Houston)

Uneeda--20" "Baby Dana" Plastic with vinyl head. Sleep blue eyes. Open/closed mouth smiling/nurser. Has grow hair feature. Original. Marks: UNEEDA DOLL CO. INC./MCMLXX-lll/2171. 1975. $6.00.

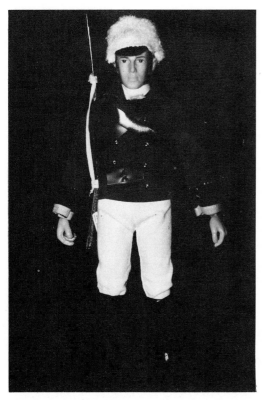

Universal--8" "Continental Soldier" Plastic and vinyl full action figure. Painted features. Marks: Product of/Universal/Hong Kong. $5.00. (Courtesy Joe Bourgious)

Universal--8" "Hessian Soldier" Plastic and vinyl full action figure. Painted features. Marks: Product of/Universal/Hong Kong. $5.00. (Courtesy Joe Bourgious)

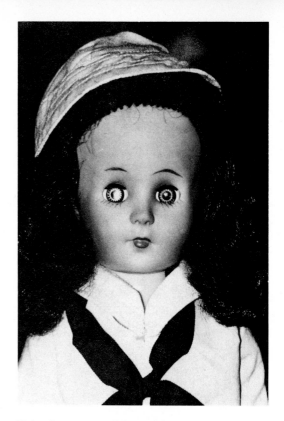

Universal--8" "British Soldier" Plastic and vinyl, full action figure. Painted features. Marks: Product of /Universal/Hong Kong. $5.00. (Courtesy Joe Bourgious)

Valentine--14" Hard plastic with vinyl head. Sleep blue eyes/lashes. Jointed ankles. Original sailor suit. Marks: AE, on head. MADE IN U.S.A./Pat. Pend., on back. Used same doll for "Ballerina". $18.00.

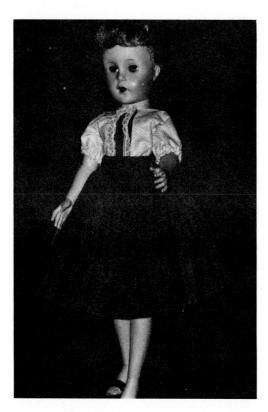

Valentine--19" "High Heel" Doll by Valentine with both names of I. Miller and Valentine on the box. Full joints plus knees, waist and ankles. Hard plastic with vinyl arms and head. Sleep eyes with molded lashes. All fingers separate. Marks: 17VW, on head. Original. $18.00. (Courtesy Virginia Jones)

Valentine--16" "Rosebud" Plastic with vinyl head and arms. Open/closed mouth. Sleep eyes/lashes. Original. Marks: None. 1964. $5.00. (Courtesy Anita Pacey)

Hi!
I'm
Ginny

And I'm
Jeanne

And together we're the Ginny Doll Club which was organized in 1973 for the purpose of research in the Ginny Doll Family and for exchange of information through a quarterly newsletter sent to all members.

We have been honored and pleased to have had the opportunity to edit this Vogue Section of Pat Smith's Volume IV. Pat has done a wonderful job on collecting more data on Ginny and Family and she has been a real pioneer in researching Vogue Dolls and in recognizing them as very collectible little dolls.

For those who are very interested in Ginny and Vogue Dolls, may we extend an invitation to you to join our Ginny Doll Club.

Jeanne Niswonger, President
Ginny Doll Club
305 West Beacon Road
Lakeland, Florida 33803

Complete information on the Vogue Doll Co. will be found in Series 1, page 295 and Series 11, page 319. Vogue used bisque dolls from Germany (Kammer & Rinehart) in the 1920's & early 1930's but the costumes were made by Mrs. Graves. It is not known if they were "tagged" with a Vogue label.

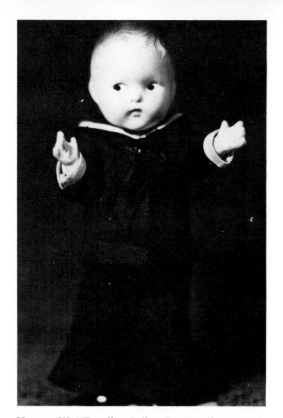

Vogue--8" "Toodles" All composition with painted eyes. Original. Marks: Vogue, on head. Doll Co., on body. $25.00. (Courtesy Mandeville-Barkel Collection)

Vogue--8" "Toodles Sailor Boy" All composition with painted eyes. Original. Marks: Vogue, on head. Doll Co., on body. $25.00. (Courtesy Mandeville-Barkel Collection)

Vogue--This is the painted eye Toodles of the 1940's in an original but unidentified outfit. $25.00. (Courtesy Jay Minter)

Vogue--12" "Betty Jane" All composition. Blue sleep eyes. Bent right arm. Marks: None on doll. Clothes are original and tagged: VOGUE DOLLS, INC. 1947. Doll made by Ideal for Vogue. Red plaid woven cotton with white eyelet trim. $65.00. (Courtesy Marge Meisenger)

Vogue--12" "Betty Jane" Shows close up of the face of the doll made by Ideal for Vogue and dressed in a tagged Vogue dress. 1947. (Courtesy Marge Meisinger)

Vogue--20" "Mary Ann" Composition with mohair wig, blue sleep eyes/lashes. Original two piece navy dress, white trim buttons and collar. $85.00. (Courtesy Mrs. E. Bethscheider)

Vogue--13" "Mary Jane" All composition with sleep blue eyes. Mohair wig and closed mouth. Right arm is bent. Marks: None except for "bumps" on back of neck. Dress tag: Vogue/Medford, Mass. Dolls were supplied by Ideal. $65.00. (Courtesy Barbara Baker)

Vogue--Shows the original marked Vogue box that the Mary Jane came in. Dress is red with blue/white floweres.

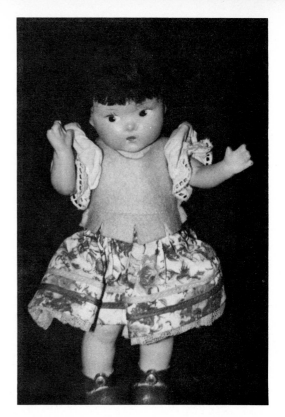

Vogue--8" "Toodles" All composition with painted blue eyes. Dressed as "Mexican" 1940's. Flowered cotton skirt. Red & yellow plaid trim. Gold felt top with white cotton sleeves. Eyelet trim. $25.00. (Courtesy Marge Meisinger)

Vogue--"Boy and Girl Toodles" All composition and original. Marks: VOGUE, on head and body. $95.00 complete. (Courtesy Jay Minter)

Vogue--"Toodles" baby with bent legs and right arm. All composition. Marks: Vogue. Replaced wig. Circa 1940's. $35.00. (Courtesy Marge Meisinger)

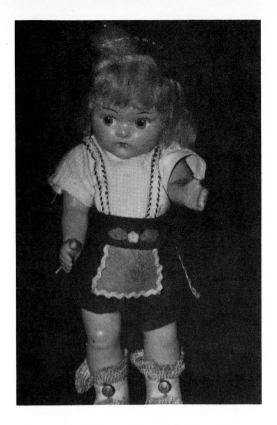

Vogue--"Toodles" as Hansel. 1940's. All composition. Pants of magenta felt with grey felt panel. White rick-rack. White checkered dimity top. Braid trim. $25.00. (Courtesy Marge Meisinger)

Vogue--7½" "Toodles" of the International group and dressed as "China". All composition with painted eyes. $25.00. (Courtesy Jay Minter)

Vogue--8" "Toodles Boy" All composition with molded, painted hair and painted eyes. All original. Marks: Vogue, on head and Doll Co., on body. $25.00.

Vogue--7½" "Toodles" All composition and dressed as Prince Charming of 1943. $25.00. (Courtesy Jay Minter)

Vogue--7" "Toodles Baby" All composition with painted eyes. All original. Marks: Vogue, on head and Doll Co., on body. $35.00. (Courtesy Mandeville-Barkel Collection)

Vogue--7½" "Ginny" Painted blue eyes. All hard plastic. 1949. Marks: VOGUE, on head. VOGUE DOLL, on back. Original tennis clothes. Dress is tagged but sweater is not. The sweater & cap are green with red balls & white/red crossed tennis rackets. Outfit 346 (1954) is shown on wrong doll. $25.00. (Courtesy Bessie Carson)

Vogue--Shows two painted eyed, hard plastic Ginny's. One is a boy and the other a girl. They are not "walkers". Marks: VOGUE, on head. VOGUE DOLLS, on back. $25.00. (Courtesy Phyllis Houston)

Vogue--All hard plastic Ginny with painted eyes. Gold velveteen coat with hood. White real fur trim. $25.00. (Courtesy Marge Meisinger)

Vogue--8" "Ginny" in riding habit. Pants are white with red jacket and helmet. All of felt. Black boots. (Author). Outfit $12.00. $22.00.

Vogue--This early Ginny is wearing Square Dance Dress #2 of 1952. (Author). Outfit $12.00. $22.00.

Vogue--This early Ginny wears Fisherman outfit of 1952. Outfit $6.00. $22.00. (Courtesy Kathleen Flowers Council)

Vogue--Ginny in outfit #51 ("The Ocean Wave" Square Dancers) 1952. Red cotton with white dots. White except hem. Embroidered band around skirt. Outfit $6.00. $22.00. (Courtesy Marge Meisinger)

Vogue--Ginny dressed as "Wanda" #40. 1953. White printed cotton. Outfit $5.00. $22.00. (Courtesy Marge Meisinger)

Vogue--Ginny as Davy Crockett which includes pin. Circa 1953. Buckskin color suedine. Hat of real fur. Outfit $12.00. $22.00. (Courtesy Marge Meisinger)

Vogue--Ginny dressed as John Alden. 1953. Grey cotton top & pants. White cotton collar & cuffs. Outfit $12.00. $22.00. (Courtesy Marge Meisinger)

Vogue--Ginny as "Nan Bridesmaid" #32. 1953. Blue taffeta. Blue net collar & overskirt. Blue hat. Outift $10.00. $22.00. (Courtesy Marge Meisinger)

Vogue--Ginny as "Alice In Wonderland" 1952. Blue cotton dress. Lace edging. White cotton apron. Outfit $10.00. $22.00. (Courtesy Marge Meisinger)

Vogue--Ginny as Bridesmaid #56. 1953. Pink taffeta with pink net collar & overskirt. Pink hat. Outfit $10.00. $22.00. (Courtesy Marge Meisinger)

Vogue--Ginny is dressed as Plantation Girl. 1953. Outfit $12.00. $22.00. (Courtesy Jay Minter)

Vogue--8" "Ginny Ballerina" Very early satin ribbon in pink hues ballerina outift. Outfit $8.00. $22.00.

Vogue--Hard plastic "Hansel" 1953. Outfit #33. Magenta suedine pants & shoes. White frosted organdy blouse. Hat is missing and skates are not original to costume. Outfit $12.00. $22.00. (Courtesy Marge Meisinger)

Vogue--Ginny in outfit #34. "Gretel" 1953. Outfit $12.00. $22.00. (Courtesy Marie Ernst)

Vogue--Ginny is wearing a skirt and blouse of 1954 with matching bonnet. Outfit $5.00. $16.00. (Courtesy Jay Minter)

Vogue--Ginny wears gown #65 of 1955. Outfit $10.00. $16.00. (Courtesy Jay Minter)

Vogue--This bent leg Ginny baby of all hard plastic is very early and has brown eyes and is dressed in original aqua/pink body suit and attached ears of an Easter Bunny. $30.00. (Courtesy Jay MInter)

Vogue--8" "Ginny Clown" All hard plastic, walker. Molded lashes. All original. Marks: Vogue, on head. Ginny/Vogue Dolls/Inc./Pat. No. 2687594/Made in U.S.A., on body. Outfit $12.00. $16.00. (Courtesy Mandeville-Barkel Collection)

Vogue--8" "Ginny" in original pink skating outfit. One piece bodysuit with her name all over it and matching skirt and cap. Outfit $10.00. $16.00.

Vogue--8" "Ginny" early hard plastic. No molded lashes. Dressed as "Alice In Wonderland" Outfit $12.00. $22.00.

Vogue--8" "Ginny Bride and Groom" All hard plastic, sleep eyes with painted lashes. All original. Marks: Vogue, on head and Vogue/Medford, Mass., on tags. Outfits $15.00 each. $22.00. (Courtesy Mandeville-Barkel Collection)

Vogue--8" "Ginnys" All hard plastic. Button reads: Hi! I'm Ginny. All original. Marks: Vogue, on head. Doll Co., on body. Outfits $5.00. $16.00. (Courtesy Mandeville-Barkel Collection)

Vogue--"Ginny" in outfit #6170. 1956. Rose pink velveteen cap & bodice. White dimity skirt with printed flowers. White lace trim. Outfit $12.00. $22.00. (Courtesy Marge Meisinger)

Vogue--8" "Ginny" All hard plastic with brown caricul wig, sleep eyes with painted lashes. Original. Marks: Vogue, on head and Vogue Doll, on body. Outfit $5.00. $22.00. (Courtesy Mandeville-Barkel Collection)

Vogue--Here Ginny is shown in outfit #6075 of 1956. Outfit $10.00. $16.00. (Courtesy Jay Minter)

Vogue--"Ginny" in outfit #6151. 1956. Blue dress. White organdy cap & apron. Outfit $10.00. $16.00. (Courtesy Marge Meisinger)

Vogue--Shows Ginny with one of her trunks. 1956. Dutch outfit #46 in 1955, which originally had wooden shoes. Outfit $6.00. Trunk $15.00. $16.00. (Courtesy Marge Meisinger)

Vogue--8" "Ginny" In outfit #6163. 1956. Yellow panties. Yellow underskirt (attached to dress). White overskirt with multi-colored circles. Yellow trim. Outfit $6.00. $16.00.

Vogue--"Ginny" in outfit #6185. 1956. Outfit $6.00. $22.00.

Vogue--Gown #6160. Black velvet bodice & skirt band. Red plaid taffeta skirt. White lace sleeves & ruffle hem. 1956. Outfit $8.00. $22.00. (Courtesy Marge Meisinger)

Vogue--8" "Ginny Ice Skater" All hard plastic, brown sleep eyes/painted lashes. Original. Marks: Vogue, on head. Vogue/Doll, on body. Outfit $12.00. $22.00.

Vogue--Ginny #6046. Outfit No. 6146. 1956. White cotton with inside of skirt lined in red. Red felt hat. Gold braid trim. Outfit $15.00. $16.00. (Courtesy Marge Meisinger)

Vogue--"Ginny" in cowgirl outfit #6156 in 1956 and #1156 in 1958. Turquoise blue blouse. White felt bolero and skirt. Gold braid trim. Outfit $15.00. $16.00. (Courtesy Marge Meisinger)

Vogue--A brown eyed Ginny in #9350 of 1957. This outfit was also for 8" Wee Imp. Outfit $10.00. $22.00. (Courtesy Marge Meisinger)

Vogue--"Ginny" in outfit #9350. Aqua polkadot cotton with white cotton pinafore effect. Circa 1957. She wears a Ginny necklace. Outfit $10.00. $22.00. (Courtesy Marge Meisinger)

Vogue--1957 white felt cap & jacket with embroidered trim. Red cotton pants. Outfit $15.00. $22.00. (Courtesy Marge Meisinger)

Vogue--Hard plastic Ginny in outfit #1456. 1959. Red plaid skirt. Black felt jacket & trim. This British Isle outfit/or the far away land series. Outfit $5.00. $16.00. (Courtesy Marge Meisinger)

Vogue--Scandinavian Ginny shown in outfit #1453. 1959. Outfit $15.00. $16.00. (Courtesy Marge Meisinger)

Vogue--Ginny in riding outfit #1311 of about 1960. Outfit $15.00. $22.00. (Courtesy Jay Minter)

Vogue--Ginny in #1364. Gold cotton skirt & cap. White cotton blouse. Black velvet waistband & suspenders. Embroidered band around skirt. Printed hem. This is Mistress Mary costume for vinyl Ginny 1965. Outfit $5.00. $16.00. (Courtesy Marge Meisinger)

Vogue--Bride dress. White taffeta with nylon net overskirt. Lace trim. Circa 1966. Outfit $8.00. $16.00. (Courtesy Marge Meisinger)

Vogue--8" "Wee Imp" All hard plastic. Green eyes & freckles. $45.00.

Vogue--An original Ginny and trunk. Pin has picture of Ginny & says: "Hi, I'm Ginny". 1955. Doll is #50. Outfit is #350. Dress is aqua velveteen with real fur trim. Ski outfit is #349 and chartreuse with embroidered trim. In trunk $45.00. (Courtesy Marge Meisinger)

Vogue--Vinyl Ginny "Ireland/Far-Away Lands" Green taffeta skirt. White lace cap & trim. 1965. $8.00. (Courtesy Marge Meisinger)

Vogue--Vinyl Ginny as Tyrolean girl. 1965. $8.00. (Courtesy Marge Meisinger)

Vogue--Vinyl Ginnys in original #103 outfits of "Jack & Jill". 1965. Gold pants & skirt. $8.00. (Courtesy Marge Meisinger)

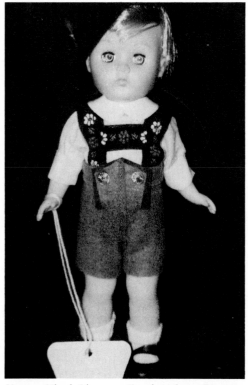

Vogue--Vinyl Ginny as Tyrolean boy, Far Away Lands. 1965. $8.00. (Courtesy Marge Meisinger)

Vogue--8" All vinyl Ginny "Africa". Brown skin with amber eyes. Afro hair. Marks: GINNY, on head. VOGUE DOLLS 1972/MADE IN HONG KONG/3, on back. $12.00. (Courtesy Phyllis Houston)

Vogue--Vinyl Ginny in the 1956 Far Away Lands Scottish outfit with red top and red plaid taffeta skirt. $8.00. (Courtesy Marge Meisinger)

Vogue--8" "Ginny Scotch Highlander" All vinyl with sleep eyes and rooted hair. Marks: Ginny, on head. Vogue Doll, on body. $8.00.

Vogue--#76658 "Hansel & Gretel". Vinyl Ginnys. 1965. Rose pink velvet outfits. Embroidered appliques. $8.00 each. (Courtesy Marge Meisinger)

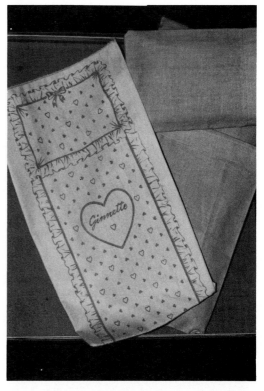

Vogue--"Ginnette's Dream Cozy" set for her crib. Fitted bottom sheet, top and spread. Pillow case. Air pillow and mattress. 1956. (1955). $5.00.

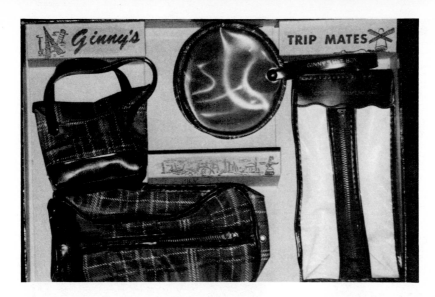

Vogue--Shows above box containing Ginny's luggage. Each piece is marked with her name. Red plaid and red plastic. $10.00. (Courtesy Marge Meisinger)

Vogue--Box top that contains Ginny's luggage. Early 1950's. (Courtesy Marge Meisinger)

Vogue--8" "Ginny" Set #1000. Plastic with vinyl head. Sleep blue eyes/molded lashes. Marks: VOGUE DOLLS 1972/MADE IN HONG KONG, on back. GINNY, on head. $10.00.

Vogue--Matching pearl beads and braclets for Ginny and ''mother''. Marks: VOGUE DOLLS/LICENSED UNDER PATENT NO. 614396, on box. Item #6834 in 1956, #1690 in 1958 & #1661 in 1959. $4.00.

Vogue--Ginny's Gym 1956. #6925. $25.00.

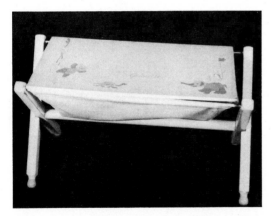

Vogue-- Wood Ginnette furniture with no marks or dates, other than name on top. 1958. $12.00 each. (Courtesy Phyllis Houston)

Vogue--10" Jill in pink skating outfit #3164. 1958. Outfit $12.00. $25.00.

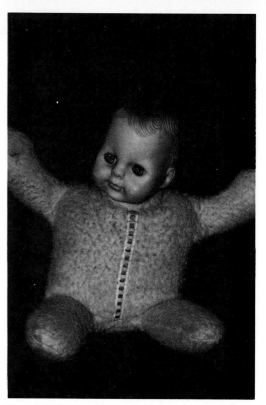

Vogue--12" "Bunny Hug" Pink plush, filled body, arms and legs. Vinyl head with sleep blue eyes/lashes. Marks: VOGUE DOLL/1964, on head. Had matching pink bonnet. $5.00.

Vogue--16" All vinyl character baby. Molded & painted hair. Sleep eyes/lashes. Open/closed mouth. Marks: VOGUE DOLLS INC/1966, on head. VOGUE DOLL, on back. $30.00. (Courtesy Alice Capps)

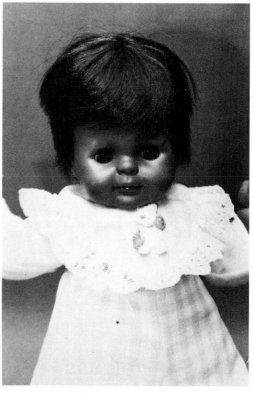

Vogue--12" "Black Ginny Baby" Cloth with vinyl head and limbs. Sleep eyes and closed mouth. Marks: Vogue Doll/1964. $6.00. (Courtesy Anita Pacey)

Vogue--12" "Little Miss Ginny" Plastic & vinyl. Pink knit dress with white cotton sleeves. Embroidered band on skirt. 1970. Marks: VOGUE, on head. $14.00. (Courtesy Marge Meisinger)

Vogue--15" "Miss Ginny Bride" All vinyl with sleep eyes. Tag: Hi! I'm 15" Miss Ginny, etc. and the dress is tagged Vogue but apparently there are no markings on the doll. $20.00. (Courtesy Renie Culp)

Vogue--18" "Baby Dear" using the same body as the original Baby Dear with back of leg marked: 1960/E. Wilkins. The head is marked Vogue Dolls. Cloth with vinyl head and limbs. Original aqua outfit. Brown sleep eyes. $20.00. (Courtesy Anita Pacey)

Vogue--10" "Miss Ginny" Plastic and vinyl. Gown is white and red. Marks: Vogue Dolls, Inc., on head. $20.00. (Courtesy Anita Pacey

Whitman--4½" "Little Red Riding Hood" Wire covered with stockenette. Painted features. Yellow yarn hair. Plastic house with paper insert. House makes a carry case. In this series also: Sally Stewardess, Brenda Bride, Mother Goose, Goldilocks, Nina Nurse, Betty Ballerina, Cinderella, Rock-a-Bye Baby. Marks: A REUBEN KLAMER CREATION/WHITMAN, on box. $6.00.

Virga--6" "Lucy Locket" All hard plastic with one piece body & head. with head tilted down. Painted blue eyes and painted on shoes and socks. Song of Lucy Locket who lost her locket printed around the dress hem. Marks: VIRGA, on back. $7.00. (Courtesy Marie Ernst)

Virga--10" "Bridesmaid" All hard plastic with jointed neck & shoulders only. Sleep blue eyes. Molded on white shoes with bows. Marks: None. Made by Beehler Arts. $3.00.

Wood--7½" All wood. Jointed shoulders and hips only. original. Marks: MADE IN/ POLAND, on foot on paper tag. $3.00. (Courtesy Mary Partridge)

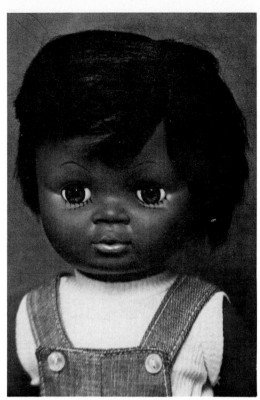

Wright--19'' "Christine" Plastic and vinyl. Designed from the Grandchild by maker, Beatrice Wright. Marks: Beatrice Wright/1967, on head. $25.00. (Courtesy Anita Pacey)

Wright--19'' "Alfie" Plastic and vinyl. Sleep eyes/lashes. Marks: Beatrice Wright/1967, on head. $25.00.

BEATRICE WRIGHT

Born in North Carolina and schooled in North Carolina, Virginia and New York, Mrs. Beatrice W. Brewington, first began (1951) by instructing 19 girls on how to make dolls. This start grew into the Beatrice Wright's Toy Co. located in New York. Her first dolls were of cloth and later she designed the "correct" looking Negro dolls that bear her name. She has created dolls that are in the price range that all Black families can afford.

As far as known, B. Wright has only produced two white dolls.

Wright--16'' "Alfie Cowboy" & "Florie Cowgirl" Aldens 1967. Plastic with vinyl arms & head. Sleep blue eyes/lashes. Cheek dimples. Full closed mouths. Girl is smiling and boy is pouting. Original multi color tops with white "Terry" bottoms with feet built in. Marks: None. $25.00. (Courtesy Jayne Allen)

Wright--19" "Juanita" and "Juan" Plastic and vinyl. Marks: Beatrice Wright 1967, on head. $25.00. (Courtesy Edith DeAngelo)

Wright--18" "Patricia" and "Jacqueline" Plastic and vinyl. Marks: Beatrice Wright 1967. $25.00. (Courtesy Edith DeAngelo)

Wright--19" "Christopher" Plastic and vinyl. Marks: Beatrice Wright 1967, on head. $25.00. (Courtesy Edith DeAngelo)

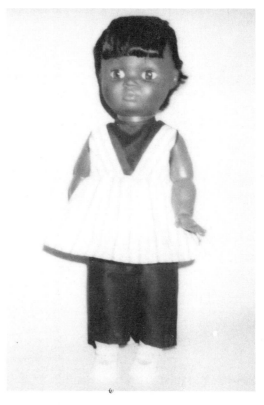

Wright--18" "Brenda" with ponytail. Plastic and vinyl. Marks: Beatrice Wright 1967. $25.00. (Courtesy Edith DeAngelo)

PICTURE INDEX

NUMBERS, LETTERS, AND SYMBOL INDEX